1020

THE RULING CLASS IN ITALY
BEFORE 1900

VILFREDO PARETO

THE RULING CLASS IN ITALY BEFORE 1900

NEW YORK

Howard Fertig

1974

Library of Congress Cataloging in Publication Data
Pareto, Vilfredo, 1848-1923.
    The ruling class in Italy before 1900.
    English or French.
    Reprint of the ed. published by S. F. Vanni, New
York, in series: Old and new sheaves.
    1. Italy—Politics and government—1870-1915.
I. Title.
[JN5449.P3   1974]   320.9'45'09   73-20130

TABLE OF CONTENTS

PREFACE

Vilfredo Pareto (1848-1923), famous as an *economist and sociologist, was a contributor to* *scholarly magazines in France and in the United* *States. Some of the letters and excerpts from* *letters which are* *concerned with the characteristics* *of the* *ruling class* *in Italy before 1900 are here* *reprinted:* *"The Parliamentary Regime in Italy"* (Political Science Quarterly, 1893, 677-721); *the* *two entlitled* *"Lettre d'Italie"* (Journal des Éconoimistes, 1887, 4ᵃ Série, t. XL, 21-3; 1891, 5ᵃ Série, t. VI, 412-20, *and* *"L'Étatisme en Italie"* (Bibliothèque Universelle et Revue Suisse, mars-avril 1897). *We are gratiful to the* Political Science Quartely *and to the* Journal des Économistes *for their kind permission to reprint the* *articles above mentioned. The* Bibliothèque Universelle et Revue Suisse *is no longer published.*

The idea that "ruling classes" rather than *"constitutions" are the motivating forces of the* *history of a country is one of the leading con-* *cepts of Pareto's sociology.*

THE PARLIAMENTARY RÉGIME IN ITALY

A marked advance has been made in the study of physiology and anatomy by the introduction of the comparative method. It may even be asserted that it is impossible to understand human physiology and anatomy unless comparison is made between man and other animals. An analogous method of studying the physiology of the social organism leads to equally important results. It is by comparing civilized with savage society that modern sociologists, following the traditions of inductive politics which have come down to us from Aristotle, have been able to lay the basis for a new science, whose progress during our century has been truly remarkable. The same method of study applied to the details of the organization of society ought also to be productive of great results. This is a truth of which M. Léon Donat shows thorough comprehension in his book on experimental politics; and perhaps the day is not far off when the inductive method will acquire the same absolute mastery in political science that it already holds in physical science. It is from this point of view that a study of the effects of parliamentary rule in Italy appears to me worthy of consideration. If only the political phenomena which are due to specific and peculiar conditions in Italy can be separated from those which are due to general causes that might operate equally elsewhere, such an investigation promises to yield results of general validity and value.

Two facts chiefly strike the observer who studies the politico-social condition of Italy. The first, which manifests itself on the most superficial examination, is the almost entire absence of political parties. The other, which to be thoroughly understood requires minute observation, is the enormous extension of the functions of the state, which reduces almost to nullity the private initiative and economic independence of the citizens.

I.

As to parties, these certainly exist, in name; but the names serve only to designate bodies of men united by certain strictly personal interests or by a certain community of temperament. It is impossible to find any real difference between these nominal parties as regards their attitude towards the political and social problems with which the country is confronted. To this rule the extremists, indeed, constitute an exception; but they are not at all numerous. Strictly speaking, there are three extreme parties, of which, however, one only is really active, namely, the Socialists. The Republican Party maintains a proud reserve, and as to the Clerical Party, it effaces itself entirely on the political stage.

In Italy there are two kinds of socialism, of which one, agricultural socialism, is indigenous, while the other, industrial socialism, is only the reflection of French and, even more, of German ideas. This latter has its chief strength in Milan, which is industrially the most important city in Italy; but it has some adherents in all the other centres of industry, such as Turin, Spezia and Genoa. The head of this party is the lawyer Turati, a resident of Milan, who publishes there two socialistic papers—a review entitled *Critica Sociale* (*Social Criticism*), and a small weekly paper called *Lotta di Classe* (*Struggle of the Classes*). This last name is sufficient to show that this party takes, in general, the point of view of Karl Marx. Turati is a man of much talent. He is well informed and active, and probably will yet play an important rôle in Italy. He has been lucky enough to make one important convert—Sig. de Amicis, the well-known novelist, who lives in Turin. The socialism of de Amicis, to tell the truth, does not go further than a vague desire for the amelioration of the lot of the people by collectivistic laws. He does not appear to have a very clear idea of the measures to be desired or of the effect which they would produce. But the simple fact that de Amicis has become a follower of the Socialists has increased their reputation and probably contributed, at the last election, to the success of the Socialist candidate, Sig. Merlani. This election is very significant, as Merlani was opposed by General Pelloux, and Turin is a stronghold of the military party. In Milan the Socialist Party presented a very clear program—the contest of the masses against the bourgeoisie. Their candidates only registered a small number of votes. Turati had 352 out of 2,569 votes, while his chief opponent had 1,458. Another of their candidates, Signor Gnocchi Viani, a clever man, obtained 620 out of 3,095 votes.

Agricultural socialism is spreading in the provinces of Mantua and Parma, and in some southern provinces, where it takes the form of a simple desire for the partition of the land. In former times its centre was in Romagna, but it now seems to have lost ground there. It was in Romagna that Cipriani, who was unjustly condemned and imprisoned by the Italian courts, was returned as a socialist deputy. Under Crispi's ministry, it was thought well that the king should make a tour in Romagna, and, to mark the happy event, he was induced to pardon Cipriani. The king was well received by the people of Romagna; and since then he has loaded popular societies with his favors, for which reason socialism is losing ground little by little. But in the southern provinces there is a real agrarian question. To understand it thoroughly we must retrace the course of their history a little.

The revolution in Italy was chiefly the work of the bourgeois, who naturally sought to turn the new state of affairs to their own advantage wherever it was possible to do so. The north and centre of Italy were like other civilized countries in that the distinction of classes was not very definite; and here it was not possible for one party of the bourgeoisie to enrich itself directly at the expense either of the other party or of the people. It was necessary to have recourse to the means which politicians employ in all countries, and which are based upon the intervention of the state. But in the southern provinces the bourgeois, without renouncing these means, adopted others more direct, which caused their yoke to weigh very heavily upon the lower classes. They took possession of the communal administration and drew from it a profit visible to the eyes of all. In the ancient kingdom of Naples many large fortunes were formerly made by the misappropriation of the property of the communes. The liberal régime has changed the form but not the substance of these usurpations. In certain places the property of the commune is leased to figure-heads, or to the friends of the communal councilors, at ridiculous rents; in others it is sold outright, and for next to nothing, to men of straw, all serious bidders being kept away from the auctions. The government does nothing to suppress these abuses, because the same persons who dominate the communal councils are the chief electors of the deputies, who, in their turn, employ their influence with the government to screen the misdeeds of their friends and partisans.

The oppression of the people in the villages has led to frequent uprisings. Racioppi, in the tenth chapter of his *Storia dei Moti della Basilicata nel 1860*, writes:

"The public land (*ager publicus*) has been occupied unjustly by the new bourgeois patriacians. And this is how it happens that a man tries to gain justice with his own hands, while they whose duty it is to administer justice are deaf to his complaints and unmoved by his prayers....Not finding the municipal representative, elected by the bourgeoisie, either very disinterested or very much concerned about social problems, the people endeavor to cut the Gordian knot by frequent insurrection."

These seditions have continued up to the present

time, and we have had some very recent examples
of them at Forenza and at Caltavuturo.[1]

The same oppression was one of the causes of
brigandage.[2] Brigands have disappeared,[3] but the
oppression under which the people suffer has not
much diminished. Here is what Sig. Leopoldo
Franchetti wrote in 1875 of the bourgeois class
which rules the Neapolitan communes:

"Such persons being entrusted with the administration of the public patrimony, it was to be expected that many among them would consider it

---

1 The outbreak at Forenza was attributed by the Minister of the Interior, in an address in the Chamber,
February 22, 1892, to the establishment of a household or
family tax (*tassa di fuocatico o di famiglia*), which is
levied or not in a district according to the pleasure of the
authorities of the commune. The deputy Gianturco, in
replying, said: "The commune with which we have to
deal was one of the richest in the Basilicata. A few years
ago the council of the commune was dissolved, the royal
commission having found that the serious charges of corrupt administration which had been brought against it
were only too well grounded; but, notwithstanding this,
the same members were re-elected."
Caltavuturo is a small commune in Sicily. The distur-
bance here, in which many lives were lost, arose out of
an attempt by the peasants to assert possession of land
which they claimed was communal property and had been
usurped by private individuals. Signor Colajanni declared
in the Chamber, January 30, 1893, that the peasants were
right and that the legal proceedings showed that more
than 100 hectares had been usurped.

2 Cf. the work of Rossi on *The Basilicata*, page 571,
where the career of Coppa, a most ferocious brigand, is
thus explained.

3 The disappearance of brigandage is due mainly to
the excellent roads which now traverse the country.

merely a means to the increase of their private fortunes; and in fact so prevalent is this idea that no attempt is made to conceal it, and when any one's financial affairs are in a bad condition it is not infrequent to hear it openly proposed that he should be elected to some office "to recoup himself.".... The people in whose hands our laws apparently intend to place the local government are generally divided into two classes: those that have followed the lucrative career of local employees, and those who, while too honest to take part in these abuses, nevertheless do not prevent their occurrence.... In this way councils and local boards, and the boards of administration of charitable institutions and 'pious works' are often full of ruined people who make an income out of the public patrimony.... The corruption of the chiefs naturally communicates itself to their subordinates. The surveillance of the communal funds gives the guardians and other inferior employees the opportunity of making a quantity of little perquisites of a lucrative kind, all of which are a loss to the fund. Every usurper of communal property corrupts as much as his opportunities allow him—that is, up to a certain grade in the social scale, when power takes the place of money.... The crown prosecutor of Avezzano, in his speech of January 8, 1872, on the administration of justice (page 29), laments the rapid felling of the trees in the district, and says that the forest guards connive at depredations; that they are so many Arguses in tracing the fagots which the poor man takes for himself, but are blind and dumb to the devastations that the rich make in the woods.[1]"

In the rest of Italy many analogous facts occur; but the politician's art in stripping his fellow-citizens is there more refined, whereas in the Neapolitan communal administration it is brutally oppressive, and is the cause of an intense hatred for the bourgeoisie on the part of the poor people. Their resentment has been ferociously manifested as often as the restraints of public force have been relaxed, and under similar circumstances we are likely to witness similar outbreaks.

The Republican Party is composed of the remains of Mazzini's party. It is not large, but it consists almost exclusively of men whose honesty

---

1 Franchetti, The Economical and Administrative Conditions of the Neapolitan Provinces, pp. 28, 29. The author is a member of the majority, who almost always votes with the government, and is inclined to exaggerate the prosperity rather than the evil condition of the country. In political and social questions, as in courts of law, the testimony most worthy of confidence is that of persons who acknowledge facts contrary to their general mode of thinking, or who acknowledge their friends to be in the wrong. It is on testimony of this nature that I have tried as much as possible to rely, rejecting the testimony of persons who are speaking in favor of their friends and against their adversaries.

and straight-forwardness are above suspicion. As a rule, it refuses to take part in the political elections, allowing its adherents, at most, to assist in communal elections only. The *Fratellanza Artigiana* of Florence, which preserves the purest Mazzinian traditions, is in favor of absolute abstention from voting. At the last elections (1892) it declared:

"It is a sacred duty of the democratic party to abstain from voting, abandoning forever a war which serves only to harden the hearts and intellects of young men, by upholding a system against which the only thing that could succeed would be an open and loyal war made by the people in the name of the people, claiming their rights. Remember, electors, what Giuseppe Mazzini said! Whoever tries to perpetuate an institution which has had a death-blow is trying to do impossibilities. Galvanic action may simulate life for a brief moment, but cannot give it reality."

At Milan, however, a circumstance occurred which sent the Republicans to the ballot-box. Their candidate, Sig. de Andreis, was not elected, but he obtained 1121 votes against 1967 cast for his opponent, who was supported by the government. These 1121 votes, however, were not all given by the Republicans; many others voted for Sig. de Andreis, as a protest against governmental corruption and oppression. These facts tend to show how utterly null is the influence of the Republican Party in Italian political life.

The influence of the Clerical Party is scarcely greater. It is said that the pope, when asked why he would not allow the faithful to vote, answered: "When one of our followers gets into Parliament we lose him." Whether these words were said or not, they are full of truth. Not only those who get into Parliament, but those who have employment under the government—and nearly all have—become lukewarm partisans. Persons well acquainted with the families of the most clerical of the Roman aristocracy maintain that if they were to vote secretly whether or no they would give Rome back to the pope, the negatives would be more numerous than the affirmatives, since these families would not risk losing the enormous increase of value which the removal of the capital to Rome has given to their houses. It is often said that when the Clerical Party does vote in Italy, a great change will take place in Italian political life. This is an error. In Rome the Clericals vote at the communal elections, and yet they do not succeed in getting possession of the municipal offices. When the Syndic of Rome, Torlonia, was removed from office for having paid a visit to the cardinal-vicar, they had not the courage even to protest. Nor do they protest now when it is proposed to hold an exhibition in Rome, and to open it on the anniversary of the taking of the city by the Italian troops. Owing to the fact that the Clerical electors in Rome are mostly small trades-people whom the exhibition would benefit, some municipal councilors belonging to the party even voted in favor of the exhibition, in spite of the date selected for its opening—an evidence of lukewarmness of which the pope complained bitterly.

This last illustration brings us close to the limits where the confusion of the Italian parties begins. In order to realize the degree of confusion that prevails, a comparison between English and American political leaders on the one hand, and Italian public men on the other, will be found serviceable.

In England and in the United States a certain connection is established between the names of public men and the ideas they represent; so that it is sufficient, for example, to learn that Mr. Gladstone has obtained a majority at the elections in order to know that he will propose to solve the Irish question; or to learn that the Democratic Party has triumphed in the United States under the leadership of Mr. Cleveland in order to infer that the country will not continue to increase its customs duties. With Italian politicians nothing of the sort is possible. For example, Sig. Minghetti fell from office because he proposed that the control of the railways should be given over to the state. His attitude on this question was not dictated by political exigencies; it was the result of a life-long inclination on his part towards state socialism. He considered it absolutely indispensable for the good of the country to take away the railways from the plutocracy who owned them; and to attain this end he did not hesitate to separate from his old companions who remained faithful to the liberal policy of Count Cavour, and thus to cause the dissolution of the old party of the Right. It would hence have been natural to suppose that his project would become the chief object of Sig. Minghetti's future efforts, as home rule has become that of Mr. Gladstone. Nothing of the sort. A very few years later, Sig. Minghetti was seen supporting a ministry, the chief point in whose program was the abandonment of the railways to private control. Further, Sig. Minghetti voted for a law which put the administration of the railways in the hands of a ring much worse than that which he had desired to destroy. Facts like these occur occasionally everywhere, but what is remarkable in Italy is that they are the general rule and that they seem quite natural. To realize this state of things, the American or English reader must picture to himself a condition of feeling in England, for example, which would make it seem natural that the day after Mr. Gladstone had obtained office, Lord Salisbury should unite with him in laying before the House some bill to establish home rule in Ireland. And it is necessary to bear in mind that Sig. Minghetti was a perfectly honorable man, and that it would not enter any one's mind that he had other than honorable motives for his change of opinion. This, of course, is not always the case as regards the changes of opinion of other politicians. It is impossible to deny that in the case of many public men the desire for pecuniary advantage or for some satisfaction to their vanity counts for a great deal in their frequent changes of attitude. But whatever may be the motive for such changes, the Italian electors appear to regard them as natural, and show no disposition to hold their turncoat representatives to a strict account. There were in the last Chamber, for instance, a certain number of deputies of the extreme Left, who one fine day decided to support the government, and who took the name of "Legitimate Radicals." These gentlemen had almost all obtained their seats as violent opponents of the Triple Alliance; but on becoming friends of the government they became all at once partisans of the Triple Alliance and delivered speeches strongly contrasting with those which they had made before election. Notwithstanding this, the same electors re-elected them. This fact alone would not suffice to prove that the majority of the electors had become turncoats like their deputies, for in Italy the government exercises a great influence over the elections; but a certain number of electors, at least, must have changed their opinions.

One result of this state of things, which is at the same time a proof of its prevalence, is the care with which many Italian public men avoid committing themselves. In order not to be embarrassed by the expression of their old opinions when the time may come to have new ones, they make a point of speaking in an ambiguous manner which recalls that of the ancient oracles. One candidate, who was chosen at the last elections, said that he could support any government which had the welfare of the nation sincerely at heart, —a declaration which certainly threw little light upon the speaker's personal convictions. Not all candidates carry the method so far; but in nearly all electoral programs phrases occur whose object is to avoid all precise treatment of the problems which are agitating the country. A candidate states, for example, that he "will vote for such military and naval expenditures as are necessary for the good of the country." This statement satisfies equally those people who believe that the good of the country requires an increase of these expenses, and those who believe that it is necessary, on the contrary, to curtail them. Another, following the program of Minister Giolitti, declares that he will not vote for new taxes unless they are absolutely necessary; which evidently commits him in no way, since new taxes are invariably declared necessary by those who propose them. A similar vagueness characterizes many recent utterances on the tariff question. By the customs law of 1887 Italy entered upon a policy of protection; yet the authors of the tariff and their friends have never frankly called themselves protectionists, as M. Meline and his adherents have done in France. They represent the new system as an inevitable expedient under the conditions of the times, and they speak much of the natural law of free exchange, which is to guide economic policy when circumstances make it possible. The lack of positive principle is illustrated by an incident during the discussion of the tariff law. Sig. Magliani, the Minister of Finance, at first declared himself opposed to a duty on foreign wheat (originally three francs on the 100 kilos, and now five francs); but when it became evident that the defection of the so-called Agrarians, who desired such a duty, might destroy the protectionist majority, Magliani supported the proposal and made the House vote it. While the question was pending, Sig. Grimaldi, Minister of Commerce, who had not been advised of any change of view on the part of the ministry, made a speech at Colle Val d'Elsa, in which he said that "the ministry would never accept a tax on foreign grain." Only a few weeks after this speech the duty on wheat was proposed by the ministry, and the bill bore the signature of Sig. Grimaldi.

Another consequence of this state of things is that, as a rule, the Italian electors have no platforms submitted to them, as in England or America. They are called upon to pronounce upon men, seldom on facts or events. There was an occasion lately (1890) when it seemed that a clear and definite question was to be laid before the country. The premier, Sig. Crispi, at least, had a program. He wished to follow a policy which was characterized as "imperial." According to Crispi, Italy was to become a great military and naval power, and was to play a rôle of great importance in the European political world. To carry out this policy the nation must make the necessary sacrifices; it must not be niggardly in bearing taxes and incurring debts. Others—Sig. Jacini in the name of the Conservatives and Sig. Cavallotti for the extreme Left—wished for no new taxes and no new debts, and preferred to sacrifice the important rôle that Crispi proposed to play in foreign politics. Here, then, were two clear programs between which the country might decide.

But, at this moment, Sig. di Rudinì and his friends of the Old Right came to the front and executed a manoeuvre which afterwards brought them into power, but which has increased, if possible, the confusion of parties. Di Rudinì and his friends declared that both aims could be attained and both programs executed; that, by economies in the budget, new taxes and new debts could be avoided and military expenditures continued on a scale which would enable Italy to take a leading position in foreign affairs. This satisfied everybody—the court, which insisted on the maintenance of the Triple Alliance and the expenditures which such a policy necessarily entailed, and the taxpayers, who protested against new taxes. Crispi allowed himself to be overreached by the Old Right and adopted the same program, at least in its chief features. The plan, however, was impracticable— a fact which its originators might have suspected but agreed to ignore. Here is a list of the expenditures of Italy during the financial year 1889-90, in millions of francs:

Unavoidable expenses (interest on the permanent and redeemable public debt, pensions, etc.)	700
Military expenses	422
All other expenses	515
Total	1,637

The last item of 515 millions was the only

place where di Rudinì's economies could be exercised. But even here there were expenses which it was impossible to reduce: expenses, for example, incidental to the collection of taxes; expenses for the maintenance of the police, etc. It could not be seriously hoped to introduce here economies sufficient to cover the large sums of which Italy stood in need. In di Rudinì's program this difficulty was simply evaded. As premier, di Rudinì was forced, in spite of his program, to contract new debts, and nevertheless he failed to reëstablish the equilibrium of the budget. Impelled by necessity, he thought of lessening the military expenses. It was then that he encountered the resistance of the court. An intrigue, cleverly conducted by an employee of the royal household, brought Sig. Giolitti into power and permitted him to dissolve the Chamber and control the ensuing elections. Minister Giolitti is maintaining the equilibrium of the budget by loans. He is openly borrowing thirty million francs a year for the construction of railways. He is also borrowing indirectly, through an operation in annuities; and, probably, he will be obliged to borrow still more on other pretexts.

There is doubtless something to be said in favor of each of the three methods by which the balance of the budget can be maintained, viz., loans, increase of taxation and diminution of military expenditures; but the politicians steadily avoid committing themselves to any one of these different methods, and the country is never called upon to make a choice between them.

Ministerial crises in Italy rarely lead to an entire change of the cabinet. It is generally a matter of reorganization; and the opposition of yesterday may become a part of the ministry it had previously opposed. A newspaper inspired by Sig. Nicotera (minister of the interior in di Rudinì's cabinet) states that when Giolitti, for a long time a partisan of di Rudinì, attacked him, the members of di Rudinì's cabinet agreed not to take part in any ministry which Giolitti might form. Two members—the minister of war and the minister of marine—did not keep their word, and took office under the new ministry. Sig. Grimaldi was one of the warmest supporters of di Rudinì's ministry; in fact it was understood that he was most favorable to di Rudinì. He said, speaking of May he made a speech in the House which was most favorable to di Ridunì. He said, speaking of Giolitti and his friends, that their change of attitude was "illogical," and that it did not seem right to him that those who had accompanied the ministry in its brightest days should abandon it when it seemed falling. He presented the order of the day in favor of the ministry, which was rejected. Consequently the ministry fell, and Giolitti took up the succession. But a short time elapsed before Grimaldi became minister of finance in the new cabinet.

A very interesting report has been published, giving the votes of the deputies during the last legislative period. From this report it appears that twenty-five deputies who, on the 31st of January, 1891, voted that they had confidence in Crispi's ministry, voted on the 21st of March in favor of a resolution declaring that the House had entire confidence in his successor, di Rudinì. There were only twenty-three members out of five hundred and eight who were constant in voting against Crispi's ministry and were afterwards constant in supporting that of di Rudinì. This is a small number to constitute a real party. But what is more remarkable is to see how even the members of Crispi's cabinet voted when di Rudinì had overturned the ministry to which they belonged. To translate their action into English values it must be imagined that the members of Lord Salisbury's cabinet, directly after having fallen from power, should vote, all but one, in favor of a Gladstonian ministry, and that their electors should think it perfectly natural for them to do this.

The political condition of Italy to-day is in some degree analogous to its social condition in the time of the *Compagnie di Ventura*. Then the cleverest or most fortunate leader drew round him the strongest bands; now the politician from whom the greatest advantages can be expected attracts the greatest number of deputies, who abandon him without scruple for any other leader who seems better able to serve their interests; and sometimes they abandon him from mere love of change. Matters have been at their worst, in this regard, since the ministry of Depretis. Cynical and corrupt, Depretis destroyed the last remaining vestiges of parties; and it was then that the name "Transformists" was coined to designate the politicians of the new era. Politically, the Italian Transformists correspond to the French Opportunists; and it is worthy of note that at nearly the same time when Opportunism appeared in France and Transformism in Italy, the old lines between Whigs and Tories began to disappear or to shift considerably in England. It would almost seem as if the same causes had been operative in the three countries—with different degrees of intensity, indeed, and with results varying by reason of differences in character and institutions.

Several leading Italian politicians have tried to modify this situation, but their efforts have completely miscarried. We must note, first of all, the attempts which have been made to promote the organization of parties through changes in the electoral law. The law of December 17, 1860, was based upon a property qualification. The system was modified by the law of September 24, 1882, which considerably augmented the number of electors.[1] It was hoped, by interesting a larger number of persons in the political life of the country, to form large political parties. With the same end in view the *scrutinio di lista*, or election by general ticket, was introduced; the kingdom being divided into electoral districts or "colleges," in each of which from three to five deputies were to be chosen. In the districts electing five deputies provision was made for minority representation through the system of the limited vote, each voter being allowed to write but four names on his ballot. This law was born under bad auspices. Its

---

1 The first general election took place January 27, 1861. The Kingdom of Italy did not then include Venice or Rome. The elections of October 22, 1865, were completed by the elections of November 25, 1866, in the province of Venice. Finally the elections of November 20, 1870, included the province of Rome. The following table shows the total number of qualified electors under the law of 1860, and the extent to which they participated in the elections:

	Entitled to Vote	Actually Voting	Percentage
January 27, 1861	418,696	239,583	57.22
October 22, 1865	504,263	271,923	53.92
March 10, 1867	498,208	258,243	51.83
November 20, 1870 . .	530,018	240,974	45.47
November 8, 1874 . .	571,939	318,517	55.69
November 5, 1876 . .	605,007	358,158	59.22
May 16, 1880	621,896	369,627	59.44

approval in the committee of the Senate was obtained by a bargain, as a result of which the state bought the Venetian railways. As far as the constitution of parties was concerned, the results were absolutely null. It was not unusual to see three candidates of nominally diverse parties unite and the electors would vote for this incongruous list without the least scruple. It was therefore resolved to return to the *scrutinio uninominale*, or district ticket, which was reëstablished by the electoral laws of March 5, 1891, and June 18, 1892. The elections of November 6, 1892, were governed by these later laws, but the results were precisely the same as at the antecedent elections.

It has also been proposed to give greater authority to the Senate by changing the manner of selecting Senators.[1] The Marquis Alfieri, who represents the liberal traditions of Count Cavour, is one of the most active promoters of this reform; but for the moment it is impossible to foresee whether the proposal will be adopted, or what result it would produce.

---

1 Senators are appointed by the king and for life. They must be over forty years of age, and are selected from among the ecclesiastical dignitaries and those who have held important political positions, appointive or elective. Eligible also are members of the Academy, five years after nomination, men of scientific eminence, and persons who for three years have paid three thousand francs a year in direct taxes. Besides these the princes of the royal family form a part of the Senate.

Of late years a certain number of eminent men have tried to draw up programs which might serve to rally and consolidate parties. Sig. Cavallotti, the recognized leader of the extreme Left, who undoubtedly represents the highest aims and clearest ideas of this group, drew up such a program under the name of *Patto di Roma* (1890). It was complete and practical, and might well have served to solidify the Radical Party; and, in fact, the candidates claiming to belong to this party went before the country in 1890 with this program. But after the elections they soon ignored it, and left their leader alone with a few faithful adherents.

In 1889 an excellent platform for a Liberal-Conservative Party was drawn up by Senator Jacini, since deceased. Jacini had been minister several times, and had a profound knowledge of the political life of the country. In 1891 he still thought the circumstances favorable for the establishment of such a party, but indicated that he had little hope of its formation. In a pamphlet entitled *The Conservative Strength of New Italy* (Florence, 1891), he wrote:

"All the old parties have disappeared except the extreme Left (which up to the present time is not united), and no new parties have been formed. There are some groups, some partisans, some ministerials at any cost, no matter who may be in the government, but nothing more. This is certainly a condition of things favorable to the formation of a party such as we have spoken of.... But the character of the Conservatives is anything but energetic, and one must not ask of them what they have not the strength to give. Left to themselves, although the present circumstances favor them, they would not succeed in constituting a militant party. The difficulty is increased by the fact that no man capable of becoming their head is to be found in their ranks."

At the time of the last general elections Zanardelli, of the Old Left, made a speech in which he suggested a very logical basis for a division of parties. He thought that they should group themselves according to the greater or less extension which they were willing to give to the functions of government. But all such proposals have been treated as pure theory. Neither the politicians nor the electors have shown any interest in them. The politicians and their constituents have more direct, more pratical and above all more personal ends in view. The electors ask the candidate what he will do for them; and the deputy puts the same question to the ministry that solicits his support.

Sig. Bonghi, a leading man of letters, attributes

his defeat at the last elections, not to his hostility to the Triple Alliance, as the semi-official papers explain it, but to the fact that he had not occupied himself enough with the petty private affairs of his constituents. A certain Piedmontese deputy is absolutely the factotum of his electors. There is no little service that he will not perform, even to looking after the commissions of his constituents' wives among Roman dressmakers and milliners. This member holds his seat in permanence; nobody would dare dispute it. Other members get elected by paying liberally; but their position is always less secure than that of the deputies who can procure for their electors the favor of the government and of the financial companies that depend on the government. As for the opinions of a representative, these are generally regarded by his constituents as immaterial, so long as they do not interfere with his keeping in the good graces of each and every ministry. When they do interfere with this supreme duty, they are felt to be detrimental.

II.

There is perhaps no country, except England, where an important part of the economic interests of the citizens do not depend on the state; but the proportion which this part bears to the whole differs in various countries; and it is especially this proportion that we must keep in view when we wish to study the effects of the extension of governmental functions. In countries where protection prevails, the protected merchants, and those who aspire to be protected, evidently depend on the state. They can have only one aim—to take possession of the government, or to sell their support to the political party ready to pay for it by the utmost possible protection. Agricultural protection especially has the effect of depriving of their independence the class of great landed proprietors, who would otherwise be in a position to conduct themselves with entire freedom in political questions.

Some states, besides protecting through customs duties, pursue a policy of a financial protection which puts most of the enterprises of the country in their power, mainly through the medium of chartered banks, or state banks of issue. Accessory protection must also be considered; such as steamship subsidies, the monopolies accorded to private individuals, the privileges of the *crédit foncier*, etc. All these forms of governmental interference are found united in Italy; and if they do not produce greater evils than those actually existing, it must be ascribed to a happy moderation in the Italian character which prevents the government from taking as much advantage of its

power as it might or as much as other governments do. On studying this question more deeply,
it is impossible not to be struck with the absolute
economic dependence of the citizens on the state.
In England, manufacturers, agriculturists and
merchants hope to make their fortunes by their
own labor and not through the favors of the
state. France, even, which is one of the countries
that in this respect resembles Italy, has several
branches of national production which are satisfied with asking the state not to injure them. The
large wine producers, the silk manufacturers and
dyers of Lyons, the manufacturers of *articles de
Paris*, etc., expect nothing from the state except
that it should not prevent them from selling their
products abroad, by provoking retaliation through
absurd customs duties. But in Italy the proportion
of independent producers is far smaller. There
are many silk weavers and wine producers, but
that is all. The other producers either enjoy or
seek state protection.

In Italy, as in France, the railway companies
are closely dependent on the state. In Italy the
railways have reverted to the state, which has
leased them to private companies. These leases
are marked by a great defect. A fixed share—

twenty-seven and one-half per cent[1]—of the net profits is taken by the state. Thus the railways are prevented from pursuing the method of all modern industries, i.e., to produce largely and to be content with small profits. The government is not inclined to make reductions in the tariffs possible by reducing its percentage of the earnings, because it instinctively feels that these reductions would not always be made in order to develop traffic, but that they would soon be dependent on political influence, with a great resultant loss to the government revenues. But what is more serious from our present point of view is that the railway companies derive very little profit from the working of the old lines. Their principal earnings come from the new lines which their contracts with the government have allowed them to construct. This puts them in strict dependence on the government, which they are obliged to propitiate in order to be able to make contracts that will be advantageous in the future.

The Bank of France is closely connected with the government, but it is never seen using its influence to aid enterprises protected by the government. Of the corresponding institutions in Italy

---

1 This is the proportion paid by the chief lines. There is besides a set of lines called secondary, where the companies receive only half of the gross profit, but receive besides a fixed subsidy of 3,000 francs per kilometer.

the same cannot be said. For example, in the monthly balance sheet of the banks of issue published by the government there may be read a note explaining the surplus circulation of the *Banca Nazionale*. The balance sheet of March 31st contains the following: "Assets, 64,793,125 francs: represented by 11,043,125 in notes of the Bank of Rome; 3,750,000 subsidy to the province of Cagliari; 50,000,000 extraordinary issue to the banks of Turin." Each of these items calls for some words of explanation. Why did the *Banca Nazionale* keep in its coffers the notes of the Bank of Rome, instead of paying them out as change? As has now been abundantly proved, the government knew from the report of the inspectors, presented in 1889 by Senator Alvisi, that the Bank of Rome had a secret circulation of twenty-five millions. It was to aid in preventing the discovery of this fact that the *Banca Nazionale* was required to retain the notes of the Bank of Rome. As for the subsidy to the province of Cagliari, that was given when the savings bank of this province, whose director was a member of the majority, became bankrupt. The director was tried and convicted by the court of assizes of Genoa. In the course of his trial he said: "I am convicted simply because fortune has not favored me. Many other banks do what mine has done, only success up to the present saves them." Recent revelations with regard to the Bank of Rome show that these words were prophetic. The subsidy to the banks of Turin was given chiefly to the Tiberina Bank to prevent it from failing. It was on this occasion that the government permitted the banks to refuse redemption of their notes, and this was the origin of the present financial crisis in Italy.

These are facts which cannot be denied. It may be objected that up to the present time proofs are wanting that the banks of issue provided the government with funds for election expenses. It is certain that the government spends for the elections much more than its secret service fund can place at its disposal, but this does not prove that the banks provide the rest. Other enterprises dependent on the government may also render assistance. Companies which receive, or hope to receive, subsidies, privileges, monopolies, make good use of their funds in sustaining a government which promises them favors. There are reports that in the last elections the gratitude of certain persons who were made Senators was manifested in offers of funds to the government for election purposes. But here, too, proofs are wanting. It is probably from fear of eliciting too much information on the means employed by the government and its allies in obtaining money that the proposed parliamentary inquiry into the Bank of Rome has been stifled.

Many enterprises are supported only by continual renewals of their bills, discounted by the banks of issue; and naturally the discount is most freely granted to those which enjoy the favor of the government. It should be noted that the legal tender quality of the bank notes is granted only for a very short time, generally six months or a year. This has kept the banks in strict dependence on the government and the legislative power. To secure their good will the banks have been obliged to have what is called a political portfolio. This name is given to bills discounted to legislators or influential journalists, which are renewed indefinitely.

As to the sort of protection which I have called accessory, one example will suffice. On the 21st of last February Deputy Colajanni, speaking upon the subsidies to be granted to the General Navigation Company, said:

"The honorable Sig. Bettolo has enumerated the causes why the dividend of the General Navigation Company amounted to only five per cent, while other private companies paid twice and even three times as much. He said that the General Navigation Company spent more for coal, and also that their general expenditure was greater.... While other companies pay twenty francs a ton for their

coal, the General Navigation pays thirty francs...
Why does the General Navigation spend so much
in coal, when it might spend some millions less?
It seems that the contractors and brokers of the
company are most fortunate people."

Sig. Colajanni then proceeded to point out
similar abuses in the repairs of the steamers
belonging to the company.

These details illustrate the very wide diffusion
of gains resulting from the protection granted by
the state. Those who nominally enjoy the profit
are obliged to share it with a great number of
auxiliaries. An immense governmental patronage
has been developed, like that which existed in the
later period of the Roman Republic. Every enter-
prise enjoying governmental protection has a
great number of hangers-on. These share the
gains, and it is their duty to defend with all their
might the privileges from which the gains are
derived. As in ancient Rome, therefore, the political elections are largely controlled by those who
are indirectly interested in government contracts.

If now we leave the economic field and consider the other fields of social activity, we still
find the influence of the state preponderant. One
domain alone is free from it—that of religion.
The dissensions between the papacy and the mon-
archy have luckily put the clergy beyond the influence of the government. This is the real reason

why the Italian politicians are so hostile to the papacy. Foreigners who attribute this hostility to anti-religious feeling make a great mistake. It cannot be denied that such a sentiment exists among some adversaries of the papacy, but the great majority of the politicians have no strong feeling either for or against religion. They simply feel regret at not having the influence of the clergy on their side to consolidate their authority. Many very honorable men have a similar feeling, which seems to them purely patriotic; they wish to see the papacy use its influence in behalf of the Italian fatherland;[1] but they do not generally distinguish the welfare of their country from the

---

1 On this subject there has appeared a very singular pamphlet by G. Toscanelli, entitled: Religion and Country attacked by the Pope. Should Italy Defend Herself? (Florence, 1890.) Signor Toscanelli, a member of Parliament, was a good Catholic. He was deputed by Signor Depretis to negotiate an arrangement with the pope. Depretis, a great purchaser of consciences, wished to have those of the Catholic priests in his service. (Signor Crispi also, according to what Toscanelli tells us, was in treaty for an arrangement with the pope.) The pope, however, was not to be persuaded. The spirit in which Sig. Toscanelli writes is indicated by the following passages: "The present contemporary politics of the pope ought to be taught, analyzed and censured in the upper schools" (p. 104). "In order to wrestle with the policy of the pope, the state has three methods. One consists in not granting him the temporal power. This means is not at all efficacious.... Another is that of refusing to recognize any pope who is not proposed by the government, and punishing him if he exercises any acts of jurisdiction" (p. 110).

welfare of their own particular party. The laws which their Parliament makes give them full control of every one's body, and by means of the clergy they would like to reach the soul also. Many desire a concordat like that concluded by Napoleon I.

In default of the church there remain the schools. In America and England university professors are absolutely independent. In France they are beginning to be dependent upon the government; but a certain number of *savants* escape its control, thanks to a reputation which enables them to do without its favors. In Italy these exceptions are extremely rare: nearly all the higher instructors are completely dependent on the government. Even in the educational institutions which are supported by the provinces the teaching staff is not free from governmental interference. At Bari, for example, there is a higher commercial school which is a local institution. Its director, until recently, was Sig. Pantaleoni, a very distinguished economist, whose writings are as well-known abroad as in Italy. Sig. Pantaleoni had published a scientific study on the drawbacks of alcohol, in which he pointed out the inconveniences which the interference of the deputies had caused in this matter. This study, which appeared in the *Giornale degli Economisti*, passed unnoticed; but being quoted by a foreign magazine,[1] it aroused the attention and the resentment of the government. The president of the council of the school at Bari wrote to Sig. Pantaleoni complaining that he had set the government against them, "while he knew the school had need of its help." Sig. Pantaleoni was subjected to an inquiry, and a vote of censure was passed on him. To this he naturally refused to submit, and consequently lost his place. Sig. Bonghi has been subjected to a similar inquiry on account of two newspaper articles. Bonghi, it is true, is no longer a professor; he is a councilor of state; and this, though it cannot justify, may at least serve as a more plausible pretext for the proceedings against him. Let me hasten to add that such cases are rare. The government generally has no need to punish an independence which is quite exceptional; it only takes care to proportion its rewards to the zeal shown in serving it.

The influence of the government extends also to the courts of justice. In Italy, as in England and France, there are no absolutely independent courts, such as are found in the United States. But even where the courts are legally dependent upon the government (as in England, where they are the creatures of Parliament), complete judicial independence may in fact exist. In examining the

---

[1] In an article by the present writer, in the *Revue des Deux Mondes,* October 15, 1891.

condition of the Italian judiciary, we must rigidly reject all testimony which appears to be dictated by personal or party hostility. But unfavorable evidence proceeding from persons friendly to the existing régime, and above all, from the judges themselves, seems conclusive. An official journal has recently treated the question with unusual frankness. It begins by observing that for some time past public opinion has regarded the judiciary as less impartial than it ought to be, and it adds:

"The fault is to some extent general. It is in the parliamentary system, the deputies, the government, the press; in short, it lies with all those who have mined out of the rock of justice a vein of personal benefit. Once upon a time the judges were obliged to bow to one strong tyrant only; now they are subjected to the will of thousands, and in their own interest they must submit to the influence of great and small. Look at the struggle among the judges, from the praetorships[1] of the small provinces up to the ordinary tribunals and the courts of appeal. Study the psychology of their most legitimate ambitions; rebuild the history of their dreams, encouraged by the smiles of the syndics, protected by the prefects for the sake of their electoral influence, or lighted by

1 [The Italian *pretore* corresponds closely to the French *juge de paix*.—Eds.]

the benevolent smiles of the legal deputies, from whose small golden medals at audiences shine promises of recommendation for promotion and change of place. Let us turn even to the highest step of the ladder and read the inmost thoughts of the magistrate who, either by tact or by open complaisance and obedience to the government, becomes a political leader instead of a chief dispenser of justice. They begin with compromise and finish by surrendering. The best, seeing that the most pliable are so often preferred to them, get disgusted and leave the profession. Thus the intellectual level of the judiciary tends to decline."

In Italy the government cannot remove a judge from office or degrade him, but it may assign him to another tribunal of equal or higher rank. The government rewards its friends by promotion and punishes its enemies by transferring them from courts situated in the principal towns to smaller and less desirable places. In France the judicial tenure is legally secure, both as to grade and as to residence. It has recently been proposed to change the rule as to residence and empower the government to transfer the judges. It was frankly admitted by the Opportunist press that this proposal was made with a view of increasing the influence of the government over the judiciary. In Italy a minister of the Right, Sig. Vigliani, tried to take the judiciary out of politics by protecting it against the government. He caused a royal decree to be issued, October 3, 1873, establishing rules for the transfer of judges to new residences. But in less than five years (January 3, 1878) another decree was issued at the instance of a minister of the Left, abolishing these rules; and since then the judges have been subject, in this matter, to the absolute power of the ministry. Attorney General La Francesca observes on this subject:

"The removal of a magistrate from one place to another injures him financially; destroys his ties of friendship, his habits and his dignity; disturbs and troubles the security of his mind, and undermines his liberty. The practical result of such things indicates why they are done. We have seen justice grow torpid under the influence of removals.[1]"

These words are especially significant because of the official position held by the writer. Still more significant is an utterance of Sig. Eula, who holds one of the highest positions in the judiciary of the kingdom—that of president of the court of appeals at Turin. Sig. Eula said publicly to Sig. Zanardelli that he commended him for not having asked the judges to render him, while on the road

---

1 Del Pubblico Ministero nell'Ordine Giudiziario (Naples, 1880).

to the ministry, those services that his predecessors had required.

Sig. Minghetti, whose optimistic view of Italian politics has already been referred to, laid great stress on the growing dependence of the judiciary. He wrote:

"It would be difficult to furnish proofs of the interference of the deputies in the nomination of judges, but it is one of those notorious things of which the public conscience is a witness. Some facts, however, we can cite, which show that this thing is not regarded as forbidden or irregular. A deputy, with real but unusual candor, defended himself against the troublesome attacks of a newspaper that accused him of begging the ministry to exile the judges of his province from the tribunal, by answering: 'How could they make such an unaccountable charge? To contradict it, it is enough to say that the tribunal is such as it is thanks to me. Many of the judges who compose it were especially suggested by me to the ministry.'[1]

Sig. Minghetti also quotes an appeal sent to the ministry of justice, bearing the signatures of several deputies, asking him to select a protégé of theirs for the place of attorney general. He adds:

"In the investigation of crimes and the search

---

[1] Minghetti, Political Parties and their Interference with Justice and Administration (1881).

for their authors, judges have often paused and drawn back when they found before them powerful criminals and accomplices. The first to be corrupted by the local influence has been the government; not for money, it is true, but for votes.... Hence, old and worthy men express the fear, and some venture the assertion, that under the Italian governments from 1815 to 1860 justice was better administered and the judges as a class were more respectable than is the case to-day. I do not agree with this opinion. However, if one wishes to be impartial he must acknowledge that, where there was no question of politics, the courts of that period generally sentenced with sufficient authority."

A politician on the other side of the House, Sig. Baccarini, who was one of the leaders of the Left, in a speech delivered May 16, 1886, alluded to "the discredit into which the courts have fallen." On the 26th of May, Sig. Cavallotti cited a letter in which Sig. Baggiarini, Attorney General in the Court of Appeals, tendered his resignation, and in which he stated as his reason for resigning that he was not willing to render the government services which were against his conscience.[1]

---

1 Here is part of the letter: "I hoped to die in this career to which I was bound by ties of love, habit and study. I was obliged to abandon it when I was expected to give what the dignity of my robe and the conscience of a magistrate forbade my giving."

The trial of Strigelli at Turin in 1884 was a case in which serious pressure was shown to have been exercised by the government. Strigelli, who was accused of having forged bank-notes, was under the protection of the prefect of Turin; and this prefect, who was an excellent electoral agent of Depretis' ministry, obtained from the government almost anything that he wished. Sig. Noce, who had been attorney general of the court of appeals at Turin, gave evidence in court that his substitute, Sig. Torti, had been persecuted by the government because he had the courage to prosecute agents of the police. A letter written by the prefect was produced in court, the purpose of which was to prevent the case against Strigelli from being pushed through.[1] Strigelli was sentenced to penal servitude.

---

1 The letter of the prefect (Casalis), which was read in court on the 25th of January, contained the following sentence: "It is useless for me to point out how seriously I desire that Strigelli should not have the smallest annoyance." Sig. Noce deposed: "The officials charged with the prosecution insisted that we should proceed, it not being possible to construct a case without implicating Strigelli. Then I went to Rome and explained the situation to the keeper of the seals. I said that the prefect, although he had no guarantees in his favor, had a great interest in that man." This time Sig. Noce accomplished nothing. But he adds: "I returned a second time to Rome, and Sig. Zanardelli... told me to go ahead." We must bear in mind that the question was one of forgery, and that the prefect knew the judicial antecedents of the accused man, which were absolutely deplorable. Strigelli, taking advantage of the protection of the prefect, was

I might cite other cases, but these seem sufficient. I will only add the evidence of a judge of high position, Sig. Carlo Lozzi, President of the Court of Appeals. In a pamphlet which was published at Bologna in 1883,[1] he observes that judges are not as independent as they ought to be, and alludes to the undue influence exercised by deputies who are members of the bar.[2] He speaks of scandalous promotions, which are attributed by public opinion to political protectors; and removals which are said to have been obtained by legal deputies because they would have lost or feared to lose a case by the decision of a particular judge, so that it was needful to send him away at any cost. Let the first president, Senator Paoli, tell what happened among the persons employed

---

afterwards an accomplice in the robbery of a goldsmith named Lacarini, and had some innocent people condemned as guilty. When all was discovered, the police offered 2,500 francs to Lacarini if he would withdraw the accusation.

1   Carlo Lozzi, The Magistracy before the new Parliament. Observations à propos.

2   In the *Corriere di Napoli* of March 13, 1893, the following correspondence from Palermo appeared: "To-day a civil suit was to be argued before the court of appeals, in which Crispi was defending one of the parties.... Some of Crispi's friends made a demonstration in his favor—a demonstration so energetic that the lawyer for the opposite side had to suspend his address because of the cry: 'Let Crispi speak.' The president of the court of justice had not the courage to clear the hall; he bowed to Crispi's power and the suit was brought to a conclusion *without further argument!*"

in the court of appeals in Florence, without his knowledge, and one may almost say, in spite of him.

The men who govern the country have almost unlimited power to protect and enrich their friends and to ruin their enemies[1]—*parcere subjectis et debellare superbos*—but they do not often take full advantage of their authority. Apart from some exceptional cases (as when the Left came into power in 1876), the men who alternately hold and lose authority respect each others' friends and partisans. This is a consequence of that moderation which is a distinct feature in the Italian character. It is also a policy dictated by intelligent self-interest. The minister of to-day spares the partisans of his predecessor that his own partisans may afterwards be spared by his successor. But any attempt at organized opposition, not against this or that particular ministry but against the present system of government, would be promptly and unsparingly crushed. To

---

1 When it is desirable to get rid of common people who displease the authorities, they are usually condemned for resistance to the officers of the police. It is easy for the latter to provoke this crime, and in case of necessity they falsify facts. It is particularly of late years that this device has been employed. The number of offences of this sort reported to the courts in 1880 was 110; 1881, 7,904; 1882, 8,033; 1883, 8,763; 1884, 9,560; 1885, 661; 1886, 10,152; 1887, 10,669; 1888, 10,669; 1889, 10,204; 1890, 11,437.

wish for a part of the favors dispensed by the state is deemed a legitimate ambition, which may be combated but cannot reasonably be punished; but to wish to arrest the flow of its favors altogether, is considered an act of rebellion which deserves chastisement. In this matter even indifference is culpable. There is no place in Italy for a citizen who, to preserve his independence, refuses to be a party to politicial patronage. He finds himself in about the same position as a Hindoo who has no caste. He is an outlaw, a man whom everyone can attack. If a lawyer, he has no clients; if an engineer, nobody employs him; if a merchant or tradesman, he is ruined; if a land owner he is exposed to petty annoyances from prefects and syndics. Every door is closed to him, everyone repulses him, until the day comes when the government does him the honor to think him dangerous, and then it finds some way to have him condemned by a court of justice for an imaginary crime.

The government justifies all this by saying that these people are generally factious. There is some truth in the statement. In countries where legal resistance is impossible, popular discontent tends to faction and ends in sedition. Of all the numerous changes of ministry in Italy, none has been due to a spontaneous expression of public opinion. A movement like that of the Cobden Club in England for free trade, or like that which forced the Reform Bill through Parliament, is absolutely impossible in Italy. The government has at its call friends powerful enough to crush any movement of this sort as soon as it seems to acquire any importance. There was never a more unpopular tax in Italy than the grist tax (*macinato*). The popular discontent aroused by this tax offered a unique occasion for a great political league, such as are formed in the United States and in England. Such a movement was at first attempted; but the government dissolved the society that had originated it and the movement was at once arrested. Some years after, when the people had grown accustomed to the tax and had ceased to protest, the government spontaneously abolished it. The people, never having seen such movements come to anything, look upon them as absolutely vain and fruitless, and are not disposed to occupy themselves about them. Men who, when their hardships have become absolutely insupportable, permit themselves to be implicated in movements of a seditious character, will refuse to join a society that aims at the legal abolition of their grievances. They are sure that such a course would expose them uselessly to the vengeance of those who hold the reins of power and of their political dependents.

In the eyes not only of the people but of a

great part of the bourgeoisie, politics are a luxury which only the man who has a following, who has *clients* in the old Latin sense of the term, can permit himself. A father may often be heard to praise his son by saying: "He has no vices, does not keep evil company, and does not occupy himself with politics." This feeling explains a singular phenomenon, observable from time to time—the unanimous abstention of all the electors in a particular locality by way of protest against the government. A law passed not long ago removed the justices of the peace (*pretore*) in a number of small places. The electors of some of these places now abstain from voting at all elections. Considering that their rights have been ignored, they revenge themselves by sulking at their masters, not by attempting to select new ones. I once reproached a workman, who was a very honest man, for having taken ten francs to vote in favor of a deputy. I represented to him that if he joined with his companions they could elect some one who would undertake to get the heavy taxes lessened. He answered: "All that is useless; the heads will always do what they desire. The only good we can get is some bank notes at election time."

Election expenses, however, are not very large. As far as can be judged from rather incomplete information, thirty thousand francs seem to be the average for candidates who have local support as well as that of the government. If this support is wanting, the expense is naturally much greater. The example given formerly by England shows that purchases of elections are not incompatible with the good working of the parliamentary régime. The deputy who has bought his seat is sometimes fairly independent of the government and of electoral coteries. A person worthy of credence told me an anecdote that illustrates this point. Some friends were endeavoring to make a deputy change his opinions. They told him that his electors would not be content if he did not follow the government in all its evolutions. The deputy argued with them for a time, and then, losing patience, said: "Let them leave me in peace. I have paid them and we are quits, and I mean to vote according to my conscience." But such cases as this are exceptional. Generally the candidates regard this outlay as an investment,[1] and

1 *Il Corriere di Napoli* asserts that the last elections have brought quantities of the notes of the Bank of Rome into circulation in Tuscany, where before they were hardly known. I cannot vouch for the truth of this statement. But another assertion has been made which is supported by strong circumstantial evidence. It is said that during the last elections several candidates gave their electors halves of bank-notes for five or ten francs, promising to furnish the other halves if they were elected. It is certain that shortly after the elections the quantity of bank-notes in circulation, composed of *odd* halves stuck together, was so great that the financial agents of the

they wish to see their capital returned with a good profit.

Laws, of course, exist against electoral corruption, but they are never put in force. A justice of the peace and a public prosecutor in Venice, who were foolish enough to take the provisions of these laws seriously, were removed by di Rudinì's ministry, and the suit was dropped. On this occasion the newspapers openly said that it was ridiculous to attempt to punish the buying of votes, which had become a general and ordinary custom.

The support of the government, however, is more effective than money; and the most effective form of governmental interference is, of course, the appointing and removing of officials. On the 2nd of July, 1886, Sig. Nicotera, who has twice been minister of the interior, said in the Chamber that he was ready to furnish a long list of government clerks in the province of Avellino who had been recalled or had lost their employments for electoral reasons, and he added in characteristic words: "Certain things may be done, but they

---

government were obliged to apply to the Treasury for a ruling on the matter. It seems that the electors whose candidates were not successful, were obliged to stick together the odd halves which they had received; and it seems that even those whose candidates were elected, and who received the second half of the notes of which they already held the first half, made frequent mistakes in matching their half notes.

must be done well. The ministry has done them, and done them badly."

Sig. Cavallotti, speaking in the Chamber on the 30th of June, 1886, said:

"In the college of Pesaro at Cagli (of this I have documentary evidence) the communal messenger distributed, together with the electoral poll tickets, the governmental list of candidates, and added a franc for each name.... At Arezzo rates were a little higher. The general tariff for ministerial votes, as is shown by trustworthy testimony, was a franc fifty centimes."

Depretis (Minister of the Interior) interjected: "No, it was a franc at Arezzo too." Cavallotti answered:

"Excuse me, that is an error; exactly a franc fifty was the average price; I have written testimony of this deposited at a notary's office. At Modena, six francs; at Alatri, a college in the Roman district, eight, ten and even one hundred francs.... The asylum of Tutra [an asylum for the poor] receives a subsidy of 400 francs through the kindness of the candidate N.... In the third election district of Novara a paper was distributed on which was written: 'If you vote for these four candidates, there will be 10,000 francs for the asylum.' In the third election district at Milan a printed paper was distributed which read: 'Choice is easy.... We have four tried men of honor, who have procured for us the railway stations, the telegraph and post-offices, and who a few days ago obtained for us the following subsidies: 500 francs for the Infant Asylum, 500 for the School of Design, 1500 for the Charity Assembly'.... At Foligno the ministerial candidate obtained for the corporation a loan of 450,000 francs from the government.... In the second Roman election district a certain Ferri, originally from Vallinfreda, where he exercised considerable influence, had been condemned (for wounding the syndic) to eighteen months' imprisonment. He was suffering the punishment of his crime when it was found that his presence in the electoral struggle would be useful. Application was made to the ministerial candidate, and three or four days before the elections he was pardoned, and returned to the electoral community just in time to pay his debt of gratitude."

Sig. Cavallotti's party is the Left. Sig. di Rudinì, who belongs to the Right and who has recently been president of the council, said on the 16th of May, 1886:

"It is necessary to check the degeneration of the parliamentary system. The public administration, the assemblies, the schools, seem to have become parts of a great machine for getting votes.[1]"

----

1 Sig. Minghetti, speaking of the degeneration of the parliamentary régime in Italy, said: "When a deputy no

It is said that the evil is increasing. This is true if we go back to the earlier days of the parliamentary régime in Italy and compare the condition obtaining then with the condition obtaining now; but things seem to be scarcely worse at present than under the Depretis ministry.

It is evident enough that the various facts that we have examined stand in close connection, each with the rest; but it is not easy to say whether the political disorganization of Italy is the cause or

---

longer represents principles, is no longer moved by national sentiments; when he is the patron, the solicitor, the agent of those who send him, there exists every sign of corruption.... On the other hand, a ministry that is not able to bring together a majority representing some idea, is obliged to fill its place by securing the support of single deputies, who receive from it honors, favors and power." (*Op. cit.* p. 8.)

Sig. Giolitti, who is now president of the council, made certain remarks in a speech delivered February 24, 1886, which he appears since to have entirely forgotten: "And we go on creating university professors who have no pupils to hear them, employments where there is no real work to be done, and all this in order to find places for persons who belong in society to the large class of the idle and needy. Henceforward I think we shall be able to apply to our budget the definition that Bastiat proposed for the state, namely, a great fiction in which every one tries to live at the expense of others."

Senator Jacini observes that for many politicians our parliamentary régime "with all its rottenness, indeed because of its flaws, constitutes a real canonry, in which without intellectual effort or culture, but with a little rhetoric and a few conventional phrases, a little intrigue and a few dependents amongst journalists, any one can succeed in having great influence."—Pensieri sulla Politica Italiana (Florence, 1889), p. 40.

the result of the existing corruption. Strongly organized political parties would exercise a certain
control over the coteries that are formed to divide
the spoils wrung from the taxpayers; but it is
precisely these coteries that impede the formation
of real parties. Neither religious feeling nor aristocratic pride, two of the strongest sentiments
which influence human action, have been able to
prevent Italians of the highest class from asking
for places, enrolling themselves among those
dependent on the government and taking service
under politicians whom they throughly despise.
The absence of political parties favors the extension of the functions of government, because to
obtain a majority the ministers are obliged to
substitute motives of personal interest for motives
of political interest or passions which do not
exist. But the extension of governmental functions
is, in its turn, a serious obstacle to the formation
of parties. As a royalist French paper, now allied
to the republic, has said: "The people must end
by understanding that it is not by resisting the
government that they will obtain its favors."

I am inclined to think that the want of political
parties and the extension of governmental activity
are the consequences of more general causes.
Some of these causes are peculiar to the countries

of the Latin race, and some to Italy;[1] others are in operation in almost all civilized states. To disentangle these causes and discover the modes in which they act would be a very interesting task, but it is one that cannot be attempted in this essay.

III.

For several years Italy's foreign policy has been uniform; it has adhered to the alliance with Germany and Austria. The prime reason of this is the court's fear that the republican form of government may pass from France into Italy, and its belief that the alliance with the German Empire is favorable to the permanence of the dynasty in Italy. To become a minister you must accept the Triple Alliance. This is the reason that the Radicals who now aspire to power have been obliged to retract, to sing the praises of the Triple Alliance and declare themselves its partisans.

But it is not only the sympathy of the court that maintains the German alliance; it is also the feeling of a part of the Italian bourgeoisie and the interest of the political coteries. The greatest

---

1 Sig. Turiello, of Naples, has published a very remarkable study on the peculiarities of the Italian character and their influence on the political life of the country. It would be well, however, to give more consideration than he does to the economic side of the question.

obstacle to the establishment of the protective system in Italy was the treaty of commerce with France. All who expected any advantage from higher duties were impelled to favor an economic rupture with France; and with this aim they turned to Germany. Again, the great contractors for the ministries of war and marine, among others the powerful steelworks company of Terni, found it to their interest to spread through the country the fear of war with France, in order that the military and naval expenditures might be increased.

But in addition to those who expected a direct profit from the breach with France, the minds of a part of the bourgeoisie were haunted by sentiments which Senator Jacini has admirably described as "megalomania." The Italian revolution was rather the work of the bourgeoisie than of the people. Many of those who had helped to establish the new régime profited by it and became much richer. They became rich enough to think they could afford themselves luxuries; and, unhappily, the taste of the Italian middle class turned to one of the most expensive luxuries—that of glory and military conquest.[1] It was partly to satisfy

1 Sig. de Molinari has put the facts excellently. Speaking of the Italian bourgeoisie, he says: "The Italian middle class is more numerous and necessitous than the class formerly predominant, and it needed a larger opening to satisfy its craving for dominion and enjoyment—a craving

this desire that Depretis sent troops to Massowah. But this toy was not sufficient for the Italian middle class, who dreamt of great military enterprises. The governments that succeeded each other in France erred in not taking this sentiment into account; and they gave particular offense by the Tunis expedition. France might perfectly well have taken possession of Tunis without quarreling with Italy, provided it had considered and sought to conciliate the *amour propre* of the governing class of Italians. But, on the contrary, the French government seemed bent on humiliating the Italians. The German government did not commit this error. Prince Bismarck was too profound a connoisseur of human passions not to see how he could turn to account, in the interest of his country, the sentiment of the Italian governing class. By gratifying its vanity, a thing that cost him nothing, he bought the alliance of Italy and incited

which had been sharpened by a long fast. Like all *parvenus*, its members wished besides to make an ostentatious display of their recently acquired power and fortune.... They threw themselves into a path of ostentatious and expensive policy, which flattered their vanity and at the same time widened their opportunities. The army and navy were not put on a footing suitable to a great power without offering to the offspring of the governing class additional aristocratic employments, which raised them to the level of the sons of the aristocracy and, at the same time, gave them secure incomes."—G. de Molinari, Les Lois Naturelles de l'Économie Politique (Paris, 1887), p. 169.

this country to an expenditure quite out of proportion to its straightened means.

This expenditure has been defended as necessary to maintain the independence of the country. Such is the official theory, and many persons believe it to be true. But in reality the independence of Italy is not threatened by France; and if by any chance the latter country should conceive the idea of conquering Italy, the other European powers would certainly intervene, whether formal alliances demanded such action or not. This even the most determined partisans of the Triple Alliance are often obliged to confess.[1]

---

1 Sig. Chiala, writing of Crispi's visit to Berlin in 1876 to offer the Italian alliance, says: "Who, until then, had ever doubted that Germany would have considered it to her interest to help Italy if she were attacked by France, even without a treaty? Had not the German chancellor declared this without circumlocution to Count von Arnim in his letter of January 18, 1874, which had been made public?"—Chiala, Pagine di Storia Contemporanea, pp. 279, 280.

Senator Jacini, who is far from feeling the same enthusiasm for the Triple Alliance as Sig. Chiala, observes: "Germany was the one of the allies that had the strongest reason to be satisfied. Let us allow that there is precise equality among the three allies as to the obligation of mutual defence. But, coming to concrete facts, are all three on an equal footing in respect to their territorial claims? Certainly not. Who will dispute the integrity of the Italian territory if we do not quarrel with our neighbors? Austria is in a less perfect position, because of the different races that live within her confines. But Germany has in view, not a vague contingency,

In 1875 Italy spent only 216 millions a year for her army and navy. These expenses went on increasing until, in 1888-89, they reached 554 millions. Since then they have decreased to 359 millions (1891-92). But this diminution has been obtained by expedients which cannot be persistently employed. Soldiers under arms have been discharged before their time has expired, and companies have been reduced to an absurdly insufficient effective force. The provisions of the military magazines, including even those on the frontiers, have been used up.[1] Military authorities say, with reason, that if Italy wishes to pursue a policy which may involve a war with France, its armament must be equal to this contingency, and to obtain this result much more must be spent than at present. But how the nation will meet increased expenditures is a problem still unsolved. Up to the present time the government has attempted to balance the budget by increasing the taxes and continually making new debts. But can such a course be pursued indefinitely? The possibilities

but the certainty of a struggle to defend the conquest it has made of Alsace and Lorraine."—Jacini, Pensieri sulla Politica Italiana, pp. 107, 108.

1 It is characteristic of the Italian political régime that it tends always to sacrifice reality to appearances. The government wishes to have an army which is strong, at least on paper. It therefore keeps up the framework while it reduces the effective force to a limit that compromises the instruction and solidity of the army.

of taxation, both as to objects and rates, seem nearly exhausted. There are many indications that an augmentation of imposts would not produce a sensible increase of revenue.[1] As to the public debt, the examples of Greece, Portugal, Spain and the Argentine Republic show that Italy is still far from the limit at which a country no longer finds loans; but she is very near the point where a future financial catastrophe is inevitable. After the abolition of the forced currency in 1880 and the loan of 644 millions of francs which was contracted for this purpose, the great book of the national debt was closed. But this only means that Italy has no longer borrowed under the form of five per cent consols. It has continued to borrow more than ever in other ways. Civil and military pensions have once already served to conceal a

---

1 Sig. Mazzola has shown, in the *Giornale degli Economisti*, that of late years the consumption of wheat has diminished in Italy. In the *Journal des Économistes*, March, 1892, I have given an estimate which indicates that the consumption of wool, which in 1886 was 68 kilos for every 100 inhabitants, was reduced in 1889-90 to 60 kilos.
The following table shows the quantity of coffee imported into Italy in quintals (100 kilos):

1887	1888	1889
142,650	140,267	135,484
1890	1891	
139,824	138,166	

The reduction in consumption is evident; and diminishing consumption generally indicates an impoverishment of the country.

loan (by the sale of annuities); and now it is planned to make them serve the same purpose a second time; and there seems to be no reason why these methods should not be continued indefinitely. These crooked courses are among the consequences of the parliamentary régime in its Italian form. Chamber and ministers are not far-sighted. They are contented to live from day to day without thinking of the future. The policy of di Rudinì's cabinet, which was rather more open than that of its predecessors, brought the country to a point where it was necessary either to submit to new taxes or to reduce the army expenses. Di Rudinì and his friends, as we have seen, tried to avoid the difficulty by proposing economy in all expenses except those of the army; but this policy proved impracticable. At the present moment the government is struggling with the same difficulty, and Sig. Giolitti is trying to escape from the dilemma by contracting new debts. It is probable that this policy of expedients will be continued as long as possible, since everybody seems satisfied with it.

A few tables will best show the financial conditions in recent years. All numbers represent millions of francs.

Fluctuations of the National Debt

	Funded Debt	Floating Debt	Total
1882	11,029	220	11,249
1889-90	12,442	352	12,794
1890-91	12,634	442	13,076
1891-92	12,768	458	13,226

Expenditure on account of National Debt

	Permanent	Redeemable	Floating	Annuities	Total
1882	401	70	47	64	581
1889-90	438	107	85	68	698
1890-91	442	106	87	69	704
1891-92	449	105	92	71	717

Communal and Provincial Debts

	Communal	Provincial	Total
1882	764	137	901
1889	1,037	170	1,207

Mortgage Debts

	Bearing Interest	Without Interest
1871	6,009	4,583
1881	6,805	5,005
1891	9,466	6,152

State Revenue, showing increase of Taxation

	1882	1891-92
State property (including the railways)	77	85
Tax on houses and land	189	191
Tax on affairs (successions, mortgages, etc.)	169	220
Income tax	193	234
Customs duties, local octrois (salt, tobacco)	492	577
Lottery[1]	73	74
Post and telegraph[1]	44	62
Various taxes (including tax on annuities)	55	71
Total regular income . .	1,292	1,514

[1] The cost of the lottery, in 1891-92, was forty-seven millions; that of the postal and telegraph service was fifty millions.

Provincial and Communal Revenue, in Totals

	Communes	Provinces	Total
1871	292	75	367
1882	391	107	498
1889	523	103	626

Provincial and Communal Revenue, Classified

	1871	1882	1889
Taxes on consumption, and similar taxes	100	149	199
Tax on land and buildings ..	127	191	202
Income from the state domain ..	36	44	47
Loans, sales of public lands, etc.	104	114	178
Total	367	498	626

These figures are a little dry, but they are indispensable, if one wants to form an idea of the state of the country. The study of political science has been too long a branch of literature; it is time that it should take as its pattern positive and inductive science and adopt the same methods of reasoning.

Let us try to form an idea of the increase of the burden borne by the country, by examining the taxes on consumption; and for this purpose let us add together the taxes of this sort collected by the state, the communes and the provinces (these last are insignificant). We shall find the totals (in millions of francs) to be: for 1871, 437; for 1882, 641; for 1889, 806.[1] This enormous

1 The budgets of the communes and the provinces are made up by calendar years (January 1 to December 31). The same was true of the national budget until 1884, but since that year it has been computed from July 1 to

increase shows us that taxes on consumption have furnished the point of least resistance in augmenting the revenues. At the same time careful investigations show that the wealth of Italy has only very slightly increased from 1882 to 1889. In some cases (e.g., corn and wool) consumption has decreased, so that it cannot be said that the increase of the proceeds of the taxes on consumption is due to the prosperity of the country; and we must conclude on the contrary that in a great measure, at least, the condition of the people has grown worse.

The straitened circumstances of the country partly account for the increase of emigration,[1] which is one of the of the most serious results of the régime

---

June 30. In order to obtain the total for 1889 I have accordingly taken the averages of the years 1888-89 and 1889-90.

1 Emigration is divided into temporary and permanent, but the distinction of the two classes in the official statistics is very inaccurate. In order to avoid trouble with the authorities, many emigrants say they are going temporarily abroad to look for work, and then never return.

	1878	1880	1882
Permanent	18,535	37,934	65,748
Temporary	77,733	81,967	95,814
Total	96,268	119,901	161,562

1886	1888	1890	1891
85,355	195,993	104,733	175,520
82,474	94,743	112,511	118,111
167,829	290,736	217,244	293,631

described in the preceding pages. It is to be anti-
cipated that the situation will grow worse and
worse. The point of least resistance to taxation
continues to be found in the taxes on consumption,
which are rendered heavier by protective duties.
The landed proprietors are powerful enough to
resist any increase of taxation upon their property; they have even been able to get the land-tax
reduced two-tenths—and this at the very time
when the expenses of the state were increasing in
an extraordinary degree and the taxes on consumption were being increased in consequence.[1] The
proprietors of houses have consented to a slight
increase in the taxation of their property—with
the less reluctance because this increase is really
paid by their tenants in the form of increased
rents. Moreover, the rent of houses as stated by
the owners is generally much lower than the real
rent, and the public authorities connive at such
undervaluations. Similar abuses exist with regard
to the income tax. A few years ago the government
published a list of the persons paying the heaviest
income taxes; and some of the returns are absolutely scandalous. Some deputies of the legal

---

	1871	1884-85
1		
Land tax (in millions)	128	125
House tax do.	51	65

1886-87	1887-88	1891-92
116	106	107
67	68	84

profession, who, judging from the style in which they live, certainly cannot spend less than sixty thousand francs a year, are put down as having incomes of twelve thousand francs or less. Those who belong to the political coteries of whom we have spoken, also enjoy a large degree of immunity from this tax, which accordingly falls back upon the plain people and on those who enjoy no power and no patronage. In the future, perhaps, under the pressure of constantly increasing financial necessity, the people of importance in the governing class may also be forced to pay. This would probably bring about a change in the policy of the country. Up to the present time the governing class has not opposed the increase of the national expenditures, because they have the means of enriching themselves and at the same time satisfying their vanity. If they had to pay for this indulgence, they would be inclined to renounce it. This contingency, however, seems far off. The example of Spain and Portugal shows that a Latin country may approach the verge of ruin before the governing class renounces the policy which has brought it there. I think it much more probable that, if a change in Italian policy takes place, it will be partly the result of an analogous change in France.

It is not a mere chance coincidence that the malversations of the Bank of Rome in Italy find their counterpart in the malversations of the Panama Canal ring in France. In both countries we have here similar effects due to similar causes. Opportunism in France and Transformism in Italy have their sole *raison d'être* in the benefits they confer on their adherents; and in the long run this system of making use of the resources of the country must lead to scandals. The first impulse is to blame individuals, but it is the political system which is really responsible. Crispi has declared, in an interview, that Tanlongo, the director of the Bank of Rome, had no perception of having done wrong. This is quite credible. In the long run, every sentiment of uprightness and honesty is deadened by living in an atmosphere which is morally corrupt. To see every one do wrong makes many people believe that wrongdoing is perfectly allowable. In France, as in Italy, the scandalous things that were being done with impunity were known to the government long before the public was aware of them. Among the ministers of both countries were men whose private integrity stood above all suspicion. Yet it never occurred to them that the first and foremost reason for which a government exists is to prevent the commission of crimes. They thought of the interest of their party, of the success of the form of government which they defended—of everything except that in civilized nations there are laws for punishing fraud and spoliation, and judges to apply these laws.

Even when the public had learned of the crimes that had been committed, the governments, instead of aiding the work of justice, tried to impede it. It was only reluctantly, under the pressure of public opinion, that it consented to allow the prosecution of the criminals; and then it placed every difficulty in the application of the law and seemed to have only one wish, that of hiding everything. It is perfectly intelligible that a statesman should try to avoid a scandal which would throw discredit on his party and the entire country. Such a sentiment is most respectable. But it is hard to understand why this same sentiment does not manifest itself when there is still time to arrest the offences which are the cause of the scandal.

As long ago as 1879 the Italian government was aware of irregular practices on the part of the banks. In a report presented to Parliament in that year, Ministers Magliani and Maiorana-Calatabiano said: "The difficulties which exist in some of the minor establishments may lead to real disasters if a serious reform of the present state of things does not take place." But the government let ten years pass without providing for anything except to obtain funds from the banks for its own political needs. Finally, in 1889, an examination of the banks was made. That of the Bank of Rome was entrusted to Senator Alvisi and J. Biagini, a government employee. These gentlemen found a secret and illegal circulation of 25,976,358 francs in bank-notes, and Alvisi wrote in his report:

"The methods of accounting in the Bank of Rome are imperfect, its issues are abnormal, its circulation is excessive and partly fictitious, the general balance-sheet is confused, the notes that are to be issued or reserved for renewal are confounded with those kept for future illegal circulation."

With this report under their eyes, the ministers took no steps, except to provide that nothing should be made public.[1] We can quite understand why the government did not deem it advisable to punish the offense already committed; but why did it not do something to prevent further offenses? As a matter of fact its attitude was worse than passive: it facilitated these crimes which it could not ignore by relieving the Bank of Rome from the obligation of redeeming its notes; and

---

1 On the 22nd of February, 1893, Sig. Maggiorino Ferraris (a deputy and sometime reporter of the parliamentary commission which in 1889, after the report of Alvisi, examined the proposed laws regulating the circulation of the Roman bank-notes) said in the Chamber of Deputies: "The president of the council [Giolitti] is not unaware that, to my great grief, the government of that time, of which he was a member and which he represented on the commission, being regularly present . . . knowingly gave false documents to the commission."

but for the courageous opposition of Sig. Colajanni in the Chamber, the government would have passed a law prolonging for six years the legal-tender quality of bank-notes, including those of the Bank of Rome. In 1891 this institution found itself embarrassed by its clandestine circulation. It did not know how to redeem its notes. The government already permitted the banks to refuse redemption of their notes as far as the public was concerned, but they still had to redeem them in making settlements with each other; this in Italian is called *riscontrata*. The government, to aid the Bank of Rome, issued a royal decree, August 30, 1891, abolishing this *riscontrata;* and so the bank was able to continue its clandestine issue. Another year and a half passed and on the 6th of December, 1892, the government presented a bill prolonging for another six years the legal-tender quality of the bank-notes and maintaining the abolition of the *riscontrata.* At the same time Tanlongo, the director of the Bank of Rome, was appointed a member of the Senate. On the 20th of December, 1892, when Sig. Colajanni spoke of the irregularities of the bank, Minister Giolitti denied that there was anything abnormal in its management. He further said, apropos of Alvisi's report: "The thing seemed so little exceptional that I must confess I never even read that report." But this was not true. Crispi contradicted the statement, and confirmed his contradiction in the Chamber, February 22, 1893, by reading from his note-book the following entry, dated June 14, 1890:

"Giolitti comes to me; we speak of the banks... The Roman bank was severely censured by Giolitti; he declared that the facts discovered in the inspection offer material for the court of assizes."

Giolitti did not dispute Crispi's correction. He replied: "I do not remember exactly the words I used, but since Crispi affirms them, it is the same as if I remembered them." Then he excused himself by saying that *he had been told* that everything had been put in order at the Roman Bank. But he did not explain why he felt no necessity for verifying what had been told him before proposing a bill for the extension of the legal tender and before appointing Tanlongo senator.

In many respects, as I have said, the Italian bank scandal and the French Panama scandal are comparable phenomena. But if the French nation is often afflicted with the same evils that trouble its brothers of the Latin race, it distinguishes itself by a great energy of reaction. It has a more vigorous constitution; and up to the present time, at least, it bears its illnesses like a young man to whom they are a momentary crisis, not like an old man who can oppose no resistance to disease. It may be that the spectacle of the immorality of a certain class, which has been revealed by the Panama affair, may produce a considerable change, at least for the moment, in the proceedings of the French government; but it cannot at present be foreseen what the change will be.

Notwithstanding the German alliance, the example of France exercises a great influence in Italy. The greater number of persons who submit to this influence do so unconsciously; but this does not make the influence any the less real. In Italy more French books are read than Italian, while German books are scarcely read at all. France still preserves in great part an intellectual supremacy over the Latin race by its literature, its theatres, its science, by personal contact, by the attraction which Paris exercises, and by its affinity of race and character. It is therefore probable that if the parliamentary régime of these nations is to be modified, the modification will begin in France and extend thence to the other Latin countries. But whether future modifications will alleviate or augment the evils that spring from the present régime, the future alone will disclose.

(Florence, 1893.)

LETTRE D'ITALIE

Le 1ᵉʳ mai s'est passé assez tranquillement en Italie, sauf à Florence et à Rome, où il y a eu quelques désordres, qui, grossis et exagérés, ont largement défrayé la chronique des journaux, et fourni au Parlement l'occasion d'une de ces discussions oisives dont il amuse ses loisirs.

La partie anecdotique de ces événements n'est pourtant pas la plus digne d'attention, ce qui doit bien plus frapper tout esprit non habitué à s'arrêter à la surface des choses, c'est de voir chaque année grossir l'armée socialiste et augmenter d'importance la revue qu'à jour fixe elle passe de ses forces. Celles-ci sont considérables, et l'on se tromperait fort si l'on croyait pouvoir les mesurer dans les différentes villes d'Italie par l'étendue des désordres qui s'y sont produits, car, pour ne citer qu'un exemple, Milan, où les socialistes sont nombreux et parfaitement organisés, est demeuré calme, tandis que les seuls faits un peu sérieux de résistance à l'autorité se sont produits à Rome où les socialistes sont en petit nombre, et n'ont qu'une organisation rudimentaire. Le socialisme gagne chaque jour du terrain et cela non seulement en Italie, où il est en grande partie d'importation étrangère, mais surtout dans la plupart des autres grands États du continent européen, où l'état des esprits est tel qu'on peut affirmer sans crainte d'erreur que tout ouvrier qui pense est socialiste ou est en train de le devenir. Il est vrai que le plus grand nombre d'entre eux ne pensent encore à rien, mais ils ne résistent guère que par force d'inertie à la propagande socialiste, ils sont comme un banc de sable au milieu du courant d'un torrent, qui en entraîne continuellement quelque parcelle, et qui finira par le faire disparaître entièrement.

Ce qui retarde le triomphe du parti socialiste, c'est surtout le grand nombre de sectes dans lesquelles il s'émiette, et qui se combattent l'une l'autre avec acharnement. Le dessein de les réunir pour un but commun: celui d'obtenir la journée de travail de huit heures, et pour une démonstration générale: celle du 1ᵉʳ mai, était donc fort bien imaginé; mais on peut dire qu'il a déjà échoué; car d'un côté les anarchistes déclarent, comme l'a fait Cipriani à Rome, que la journée de huit heures est un but dont il ne vaut même pas la peine de s'occuper, et d'autre part on a pu voir que l'accord était bien loin d'être unanime sur la date de la démonstration et sur le caractère qu'elle devait avoir.

Il ne faudrait pourtant pas croire que ce qui n'est pas arrivé aujourd'hui ne puisse jamais avoir lieu; car le nombre des adhérents aux différentes sectes socialistes continuant à croître, le terrain se trouvera tout préparé pour le jour où l'influence émotionelle de quelque événement important pourra réunir la plupart de ces forces éparses qui deviendront alors irrésistibles. L'incohérence des différentes doctrines socialistes n'y saurait mettre obstacle, car l'histoire nous enseigne que ce n'est pas le raisonnement que entraîne et fait mouvoir les grandes masses humaines, mais bien l'émotion qui s'en empare sous l'empire de certaines circonstances et dans un milieu ambiant qui y soit propice.

En attendant, la contradiction qui se fait jour dans bien des principes socialistes est vraiment singulière, sortout en Italie, où le socialisme s'inspirant de doctrines exotiques, réunit ensemble les idées les plus disparates.

Ainsi, par exemple, dans un manifeste publié à Milan, on nous parle "de l'anarchie toujours croissante de la production qui excède la faculté de consommation, tandis qu'à la pléthore et à la dépréciation des marchandises contraste l'indigence des travailleurs."

Vraiment si la production de toutes les marchandises est excessive, il devrait y en avoir aussi pour les indigents; et vouloir faire augmenter le prix de tout ce qu'ils doivent acheter pour leurs besoins est une manière aussi nouvelle que singulière de venir en aide aux pauvres gens. Peut-être est-il sous-entendu qu'on fera croître leur gain dans une proportion encore plus forte que le prix des marchandises qu'ils consomment, mais comment ce phénomène se produira-t-il, c'est ce que l'on ne nous dit pas et qu'il serait pourtant bien intéressant de connaître.

Le *Comice pour les droits du travail* demande:

"Que cesse l'état de choses actuel dans lequel les prolétaires sont rangés les uns contre les autres, soit comme des soldats à la guerre, soit dans la féroce concurrence du travail."

"La liberté de coalition et de résistance."

Ces deux demandes ne se concilient pas très bien ensemble, car évidemment la coalition et la résistance des ouvriers implique cette même concurrence maudite qu'on dit vouloir éviter. La liberté de coalition est aussi réclamée par les économistes libéraux—par ces infâmes manchéstériens, comme on les appelle du côté socialiste; du côté de nos politiciens, l'épithète change, et l'on peut choisir entre; théoriciens, utopistes, ou tout autre analogue—mais quelque nom qu'on leur donne, s'il sont vraiment dignes de celui de libéraux, ils blâmeront le gouvernement italien quand il envoie les soldats faire l'ouvrage des moissonneurs en grève, et, ce qui est encore pis, quand il met ceux-ci en prison, comme cela est déjà arrivé plusieurs foi, entre autres sous le ministère Depretis. Il est vrai qu'alors les députés soi-disant économistes appuyaient le gouvernement, ne pouvant, disaient-ils, renverser un ministère qui octroyait à eux et à leurs amis le bienfait des conventions des chemins de fer; mais on ne peut en bonne logique rendre l'Economie politique responsable de ces agissements qui n'ont pas plus de rapport avec la science qu'avec la morale.

Le *Comice* réclame ensuite une loi pour fixer la journée de travail de huit heures, une autre loi pour établir un minimum de salaire, encore et toujours des lois pour protéger les enfants et les femmes, pour assurer la vie des ouvriers et pour quantité d'autres buts philanthropiques.

Ce phénomène est très remarquable. Nos socialistes ne sont guère amis du gouvernement, qui le leur rend bien, les emprisonne quelque-fois et les combat toujours, et pourtant ils ne songent qu'a augmenter son pouvoir. Ils critiquent l'usage qu'il fait des lois existantes et n'ont rien de si pressé que d'en vouloir mettre d'autres à sa disposition. Ils dénoncent au monde entier qu'en Italie la loi sur le travail des enfants ne s'exécute pas, et ils demandent.... qu'on en fasse une autre pour protéger le travail des femmes! Le gouvernement ayant entrepris de *régler* la production par le fameux tarif douanier de 1887 a obtenu les brillants résultats que tout le monde connaît, et nos socialistes, tout en se plaignant de la misère

du pays, qui est la conséquence de cette intervention de l'État, veulent qu'on y ait recours de
nouveau et demandent qu'on continue par d'autres
règlements à faire disparaître l'*anarchie*, qui, à
ce qu'il paraît, subsiste encore dans l'industrie et
dans le commerce malgré les belles lois qu'a
enfantées le génie inventif de nos protectionnistes.

La contradiction était vraiment trop frappante,
aussi dans ces derniers temps a-t-on avisé au
moyen de tourner la difficulté. Tous ces défauts,
nous disent les socialistes, sont le fait de l'État
bourgeois, ils disparaîtront avec l'État ouvrier,
lequel seul a qualité pour résoudre la question
sociale.

L'État ouvrier, Quelle peut bien être au juste
sa nature et à quels signes reconnaîtrons-nous son
avènement? Depuis le temps d'Aristote jusqu'à
nos jours, les hommes ont philosophé pour trouver un gouvernement parfait, sans trop faire avan-
cer la question; si nos socialistes l'ont résolue, ils
feraient bien de nous en instruire. Qu'ils laissent
de côté les critiques de l'état actuel de la société;
ce n'est pas à l'Economie politique à le défendre
avec la protection, les monopoles, les privilèges,
l'effroyable destruction de richesse qui s'y accom-
plit pour les armements et les guerres, et sa
mauvaise répartition des impôts, c'est bien plutôt
aux socialistes à prendre soin de cette défense,
car notre société applique largement les principes

de l'intervention de l'État qu'ils vont prêchant. Mais qu'ils nous expliquent comment ils s'y prendront pour que cette intervention produise le bien au lieu du mal que l'expérience a fait voir lui avoir été jusqu'à présent attaché. Pendant un certain temps le remède paraissait tout trouvé; il ne s'agissait, disait-on, que d'étendre le vote politique à tous les citoyens. On s'en est fort approché maintenant en Italie, et pourtant les choses n'y marchent pas mieux qu'avant. La libre concurrence sera un fort mauvais moyen de régler les prix des marchandises et des salaires, soit, ne discutons point la-dessus, mais quelles garanties aurons-nous que les hommes qu'on veut préposer à cet emploi feront mieux? M. Marcora a dit en pleine Chambre sans être contredit qu'on pourrait écrire à côté de chaque article du tarif douanier de 1887 les noms des industriels qu'on avait voulu favoriser; c'est pourtant des études d'une Commission composée d'hommes très compétents qu'est sorti ce merveilleux tariff.

Quelle recette emploiera-t-on pour mieux composer la Commission chargée de faire disparaître l'*anarchie* qui régne aujourd'hui dans l'industrie? On devrait bien nous rassurer à ce sujet. Régler toute la production d'un pays est chose un peu compliquée et fort délicate, et les moindres erreurs peuvent avoir de graves conséquences.

Il ne faudrait pas aussi que, sous prétexte de

régler l'industrie, l'agriculture et le commerce, de rusés compères s'appropriassent le fruit de notre labeur. Les faits qui se sont produits sous le régime protecteur nous ont rendus un peu méfiants à ce sujet, et l'on sait que chat échaudé craint l'eau froide.

Le tarif douanier de 1887 n'a produit que la misère dans le pays, mais de mauvais règlements pour toute la protection risqueraient fort de nous faire mourir de faim. Il faut espérer que l'État ouvrier connaîtra le secret d'en faire de bons, quant à l'État bourgeois il ne le possède certes pas, et se trompe fort souvent en faisant les lois les plus simples. Bien loin de pouvoir songer à régler toutes les industries il n'y en a aucune qu'il sache exercer convenablement et surtout économiquement, et il ne réussit même pas à s'assurer qu'on prenne les précautions les plus élémentaires pour empêcher les explosions des poudrières, comme l'a bien prouvé un exemple récent à Rome.

En attendant l'avènement de l'État ouvrier, le Comice de Milan demande un ministère du travail, sans songer qu'il serait peut-être mieux de diminuer que d'augmenter le nombre des fonctionnaires que le pays paye pour l'administrer, hélas! fort mal.

Faute de ce ministère du travail, le député socialiste, M. Guelpa, se serait contenté d'une simple commission parlementaire, mais le gouvernement refusa, nous ne savons pourquoi; il y a déjà tant de ces commissions qu'une de plus n'aurait pas fait grand mal. Ces jours-ci, on a nommé une commission pour reviser encore une fois notre tarif douanier, et les journaux annoncent que déjà bon nombre d'industriels lui ont adressé des mémoires réclamant un surcroît de protection. M. Guelpa pensait peut-être à cela en faisant sa proposition, et en ce sens on ne saurait lui donner tort. Il n'est pas juste que le gouvernement octroye aux uns ce qu'il refuse aux autres, et qu'il répande ses bienfaits seulement sur les industriels et les propriétaires ses amis; puisque protection il y a, chacun a bien le droit d'en réclamer sa part.

Dans la même séance de la Chambre, M. Prampolini, autre député socialiste, blâmait le gouvernement de ne songer qu'à faire des économies, et voulait qu'il pourvût surtout à donner de l'ouvrage aux ouvriers en se faisant constructeur et industriel. L'on m'opposera, disait-il, les volumes écrits par les économistes, mais toutes leurs théories n'ont pas donné à manger à un seul affamé.

M. Prampolini combattait contre des moulins à vent. Personne n'osa même prononcer le nom abhorré de l'économie politique. Les députés qui ont étudié cette science—ils ne sont pas nombreux—se tenaient coi, les uns pour ne pas se compromettre, les autres, parce qu'ayant voté les droits d'entrée sur les céréales, et tous les impôts, tous les monopoles, tous les privilèges qu'il avait plu au gouvernement d'établir, ils se trouvaient dans l'embarras pour donner à M. Prampolini la seule réponse vraiment efficace qui eût été de lui rappeler l'exemple de l'Angleterre, où la ligue de l'économiste Cobden a procuré au peuple le bienfait de payer son pain beaucoup moins cher qu'en Italie; et comme en Angleterre les salaires des ouvriers sont plus élevés, malgré qu'on n'y protège pas savamment le travail national ainsi qu'on le fait ici, il faut avouer que ces affreux manchéstériens n'ont pas trop nui au bien-être de l'ouvrier, et qu'ils ont quelque peu contribué à ce que les affamés eussent le moyen de se rassasier.

Quant au travail pour les ouvriers qu'on réclamait de l'État, M. Rudinì ne répondit pas que ce travail ne pouvant être payé qu'au moyen d'impôts levés sur tous les citoyens, ceux-ci auraient dû diminuer d'autant leur dépense, d'où une diminution de travail dans le pays précisément égale à la quantité que l'État aurait donnée aux ouvriers. De telles explications sont bonnes tout au plus pour un économiste; M. Rudinì, en homme pratique, se contenta de faire observer que l'État dépensait déjà 200 millions par an pour construire des chemins de fer, et d'autres sommes considérables pour de nombreux travaux. Une force irrésistible, ajouta-t-il, pousse l'État à multiplier chaque jour ses fonctions, que M. Prampolini se contente de cette lente mais continuelle évolution, bien plus efficace et bienfaisante qu'une violente révolution.

Au fond, le discours de M. Rudinì s'inspire des théories socialistes autant que celui de M. Prampolini; les principes sont les mêmes, seulement chacun d'eux les applique pour favoriser une classe différente de la société.

La machine gouvernementale que la bourgeoisie a su si savamment organiser à son profit, les socialistes voudraient bien s'en emparer et s'en servir à leur tour, mais ils n'ont garde de la vouloir détruire. Voilà pourquoi la contradiction que nous avons notée en eux de tendre à augmenter les pouvoirs de l'État qui les persécute n'est qu'apparente; ils ne font ainsi que rendre plus riche et plus précieuse la proie qu'ils convoitent. Mais ils ont tort de trop se plaindre de l'État bourgeois, car celui-ci met vraiment en oeuvre tous les moyens qu'il possède pour préparer l'avènement de son successeur. Il s'est chargé de nous donner une éducation socialiste complète, et s'il n'y réussissait pas on ne pourrait guère l'accuser d'avoir manqué de bonne volonté, ni de zèle.

Par la protection on nous apprend à souffrir que la distribution de la richesse soit faite arbitrairement au gré des gens assez heureux pour avoir pu s'emparer du gouvernement. Obtenir les faveurs de l'État devient le but des efforts des citoyens, qui se liguent entre eux pour faire tomber dans leurs mains le pouvoir, et, après y avoir réussi mettent tout en oeuvre pour le conserver, tandis que d'autres essayent de les renverser.

Aujourd'hui, le succès a couronné les efforts des propriétaires des terres à blé et des rizières, qui se font payer tribut par leurs concitoyens; mais ont-ils jamais réfléchi que ceux-ci sont les plus nombreux, que s'ils réussissent à s'entendre, ils seront aussi les plus forts, et qu'ils pourraient bien alors tirer profit des leçons qu'on leur donne, et dépouiller à leur tour les propriétaires?

Ce n'est jamais impunément qu'on abuse de la force, et qu'on donne le mauvais exemple de ne respecter ni la propriété ni la justice. Malheureusement, il arrive souvent que les gouvernements n'ont pas plus d'égards pour l'une que pour l'autre. Une magistrature indépendante comme la magistrature anglaise les gêne; ils se laissent entraîner à appliquer aux moindres choses le principe: *salus populi suprema lex esto*, et demandent trop souvent aux juges des services au lieu d'arrêts. Dans cette voie, ce n'est que le premier pas qui coûte; après, l'on se trouve pris dans un engrenage, et c'est par de nouvelles injustices qu'on se croit obligé de défendre celles déjà commises.

A Parme, de pauvres femmes ayant réclamé

trop bruyamment, paraît-il, contre le renchérisse-
ment du pain, on les a condamnées à la prison.
Il n'est que juste de reconnaître que ce fut pour
peu de temps, mais cette modération des juges
pourrait bien ne pas durer, surtout s'ils se règlent
sur ce qui vient d'arriver à Venise, où le gouvernement a déplacé des magistrats qui avaient eu
le seul tort de prendre au sérieux la loi sur les
corruptions électorales et de croire qu'on pouvait
l'appliquer même quand il s'agissait des élections
des amis du gouvernement.

Mettre en prison les gens qui ont le malheur
de dire choses qui nous déplaisent est certes un
procédé assez expéditif pour s'en débarrasser, et
si le gouvernement anglais en avait pu user envers
les membres de la ligue de Cobden, les droits sur
les céréales n'auraient peut-être pas été abolis.
Nous n'approuvons nullement la violence de quelque part qu'elle vienne, mais si vous affamez les
gens, vous ne pouvez pourtant pas prétendre que
leurs réclamations soient des plus modérées; et
d'ailleurs, même sans ce motif, les membres de la
ligue anglaise étaient parfois assez vifs dans leurs
discours. Ainsi, par exemple, Cobden, parlant le 7
mai 1834, après avoir rappelé les monopoles
qui existaient autrefois en Angleterre, ajoutait:
"Aujourd'hui les monopoleurs, agissant suivant
des principes identiques si ce n'est pires, ont in-
troduit de grands raffinements dans les dénomi-

nations des choses; ils ont inventé *l'echelle mobile* et le mot *protection*. En reconstruisant ces monopoles l'aristocratie de ce pays (maintenant il faudrait dire; ces clients députés) s'est formée en une grande société par actions pour l'exploitation des abus de toute espèce; les uns ont le blé, les autres le sucre, ceux-ci le bois, ceux-là le café, ainsi de suite. (En Italie on pourrait nommer le blé, le riz, le sucre, les draps, les métaux et bien des établissements industriels.) Chacune de ces classes de monopolisateurs dit aux autres: Aidez-moi à arracher le plus d'argent possible au peuple, et je vous rendrai le même service." Le 13 mai il disait: "Qu'est-ce que le monopole du pain (la protection)? C'est la disette du pain. Vous êtes surpris d'apprendre que la législation de ce pays, à ce sujet, n'a pas d'autre objet que de produire la plus grande disette de pain qui se puisse supporter? Et cependant ce n'est pas autre chose.... Quelle chose dégoûtante de voir la Chambre des communes; je dis dégoûtante ici, ailleurs le mot ne serait pas parlamentaire. Mon ami le capitaine Bernal leur a dit le mot en face.... Mais allez, comme je l'ai fait d'abord à la barre de la Chambre des lords, et puis à la Chambre des communes, et vous verrez que le fond de leurs discours c'est: rentes, rentes, cherté, cherté, rentes, rentes!"

M. W.-J. Fox n'était pas beaucoup plus tendre envers messieurs les protectionnistes; battant en brèche un de leurs sophismes par lequel ils prétendaient justifier la protection et l'acte de navigation comme nécessaire à l'indépendance du pays (en Italie c'est la Triple Alliance qu'on réunit à la protection dan ce but) il disait:

"Nous n'avons pas besoin de cet usage odieux pour repousser les agressions du dehors, et un moyen beaucoup plus sûr de pourvoir en tout temps à notre sûreté, c'eût été de laisser au peuple quelque chose à défendre de plus qu'il ne possède en ce moment. Il ne se battra pas pour défendre la taxe du pain, il ne se battra pas pour servir l'oligarchie qui le foule aux pieds, il ne se battra pas pour maintenir les institutions qui favorisent le riche mais qui écrasent le pauvre."

Et dans une autre occasion (au meeting de Convent-Garden le 25 janvier 1844): "Les adversaires de la Ligue recherchent tous les sales recoins, toutes les taches de boue qui peuvent se trouver dans le caractère de l'homme pour bâtir là-dessus. Ces gens qui exploitent en grand le monopole du sol britannique, vont chassant au tailleur et au cordonnier, et lui disent: N'avez-vous pas aussi quelque petit monopole; soutenez-nous, nous vous soutiendrons. Ils gouvernent avec les mauvaises passions, avec ce qu'il y a de folie et de bassesses dans la nature humaine."

Il se pourrait bien que beaucoup de ces choses, vraies alors en Angleterre, le fussent maintenant en Italie, et que la seule différence fût qu'ici il n'est pas permis de les dire en public.

Quant au principe de la propriété individuelle il faut qu'il soit bien tenace, bien enraciné dans le coeur de l'homme pour résister aux coups que l'État lui porte chaque jour. L'individu ne possède pas ce qu'il acquiert par son travail, mais ce qu'il plaît à l'État de lui laisser ou de lui donner. Les impôts indirects vont en augmentant chaque jour, les monopoles et les privilèges croissent et se multiplient; notre bourgeoisie s'est éprise d'un bel amour pour un luxe des plus coûteux: celui de la gloire militaire, et dans l'espoir de se le procurer elle fait faire à l'État des dépenses excessives dont le poids retombe sur le peuple. Un député disait à la Chambre: "les millions dépensés en Afrique ont plus contribué à donner à l'Italie une grande position en Europe que ceux dépensés sur les bord du Tibre." Avoir une grand position! Tel est le rêve de nos hommes politiques, le but unique de leurs efforts, qu'ils poursuivent avec l'ardeur du fanatique, d'autant plus dangereux qu'il est de meilleure foi. M. le sénateur Jacini a fort bien caracterisé cette maladie en l'appelant mégalomanie. Ceux qui en sont le plus atteints feraient peut-être aussi des sacrifices pour satisfaire leur passion, mais le gros de leurs partisans ne les suivraient pas dans cette voie; alors ils transigent, ils gouvernent suivant la ligne de moindre résistance, et font retomber le poids des impôts sur les citoyens qui savent moins bien se défendre. Si les électeurs influents payaient les frais de la politique italienne, il y a longtemps que celle-ci serait devenue plus modeste, mais pour faire accepter les dépenses des armements et des aventures africaines par les propriétaires on leur a donné le bénéfice des droits sur le blé et le riz, et bien mieux encore, on leur a diminué de deux dixièmes l'impôt foncier juste quand on augmentait les impôts indirects.

L'État se croit permis de mettre la main sur la propriété privée, quand il y trouve son avantage. La ville de Rome s'étant obérée pour exécuter les travaux de luxe que lui avait imposés le gouvernement, qui voulait voir sa capitale rivaliser avec celle du monde romain et avec celle des papes, on ne trouva rien de mieux à faire pour la soulager que de lui adjuger les biens des congrégations de charité qui existaient dans son enceinte. M. Crispi déclara à la Chambre qu'ils étaient de bonne prise (ces paroles sont textuelles!), et sa majorité d'applaudir et d'approuver la demande qu'il fit de suivre pour cette loi la procédure dite *très urgente*, en vertu de laquelle les trois lectures doivent se succéder immédiatement l'une à l'autre. La chambre nomma une commission qui fit son rapport en quatre jours, tout devant se faire à la hâte pour obéir à la volonté alors toute-puissante de M. Crispi. Pendant la discussion celui-ci déclara franchement que le gouvernement devait s'approprier les biens des congrégations de charité romaine, car autrement il aurait fallu demander de nouveaux sacrifices aux contribuables italiens. Avec d'aussi bonnes raisons l'on ne voit pas quelles propriétés privées peuvent se trouver a l'abri de la confiscation, et l'on est confondu quand on voit des gens se prétendant conservateurs prêter le main à de telles spoliations. Il est vrai que, par un reste de pudeur, quelques députés de la droite n'osèrent pas voter en faveur de cette disposition de la loi, mais ils n'en soutenaient pas moins le ministère, qui non seulement en cette occasion mais en bien d'autres encore substituait sa volonté aux principes de la justice, et ils continuèrent à l'appuyer jusqu'au jour où devenus majorité, grâce à son aide, ils se jouèrent de lui et le renversèrent.

C'est ainsi que sous l'action dissolvante des préoccupations de la stratégie parlementaire, non seulement les principes économiques mais même les principes moraux souffrent de graves atteintes, et que de transactions en transactions les hommes les meilleurs finissent par faire le mal aussi bien que les pires. M. Rudinì à raison: une force irrésistible pousse l'État à multiplier chaque jour ses fonctions, mais cette force n'est souvent que la corruption d'un côté et la lâcheté de l'autre, et son effet ne peut qu'étre funeste pour la société.

Aujourd'hui toute personne qui regarde un peu au-delà de l'intérêt du moment voit dans le lointain grossir l'orage qui emportera toutes ces savantes combinaisons parlementaires, comme la Révolution française a balayé toutes les intrigues de la cours de Versailles, et c'est faire oeuvre de bon citoyen et de vrai conservateur que de signaler le danger, dans l'espoir que pendant qu'il en est encore temps ou trouve quelque moyen de l'éviter.

(1887)

LETTRE D'ITALIE

A l'époque des *condottieri*, des hommes hardis
et entreprenants se réunissaient en troupe, et se
mettant au service du plus offrant, s'enrichissaient
par la guerre et le pillage. Maintenant encore de
semblables compagnies se forment, mais c'est au
moyen du vote et des influences parlementaires
qu'elles marchent à la conquête de la richesse.
On les voit de natures diverses suivant les pays
où elles agissent; fortement organisées aux Etats-
Unis, elles le sont peut-être moins sur le continent
européen, et n'ont guère d'influence en Angleterre, où l'État s'ingère moins qu'ailleurs dans la
vie économique de la nation.

Il serait fort intéressant de faire une étude sur
les moyens qu'elles mettent en oeuvre pour arriver
à leurs fins. Malgré ce qu'on en croit vulgaire-
ment, la corruption directe est un des moins em-
ployés. Si Walpole revenait au monde, il ne pourrait plus se vanter, comme il le faissait, de connaître le tarif de la conscience de chaque député;
mais il est vrai qu'il pourrait apprendre combien
de kilomètres de chemins de fer il faut leur oc-
troyer, quelles sociétés on doit protéger, quels
droits protecteurs établir, pour obtenir leur appui.

Ce sont là des moyens bien moins immoraux que la corruption, mais malheureusement d'autant plus coûteux. La morale a gagné au change, mais non l'économie.

Lorsque toutes les forces productives d'un pays se trouvent sous la tutelle du governement, celui-ci acquiert une telle influence sur les intérêts privés des citoyens, que toute la vie publique s'en trouve faussée. C'est là une des raisons qui peuvent servir à expliquer comment en Italie, où les traditions libérales du governement du comte de Cavour ne sont pas encore complètement oubliées, et où il y a beaucoup de libres-échangistes, la nouvelle réforme douanière a pu passer aux Chambres avec une opposition insignifiante, n'y soulevant presque pas de discussions, et dans le pays encore moins. Malheureusement, on ne s'en tiendra pas là; pour satisfaire les convoitises qu'on a allumées, on s'enfoncera de plus en plus dans la voie de la protection, et on arrivera à des excès, dont il semblait que la modération habituelle au caractère italien devait nous protéger. Il ne s'est pas trouvé une seule voix dans la Chambre pour demander au ministère pourquoi, même avant que les nouveaux droits de douane fussent approuvés, il avait acheté, à une entreprise qu'il favorisait, 150.000 tonnes de rails d'acier à un prix de beaucoup supérieur à celui qui lui était offert par les producteurs étrangers. Assurés de leur triomphe, par les intérêts qu'ils mettaient en jeu, les protectionnistes n'ont pas même daigné répondre aux observations que quelques rares libres-échangistes osèrent publier. Un grand nombre de députés et de sénateurs, qui en particulier se disent libres-échangistes, se sont abstenus, ou ont même fini par voter le projet de réforme des droits de douane, craignant, s'ils votaient contre le gouvernement, de compromettre les intérêts de leur parti politique, ou de leurs provinces. Il faut ajouter à cela l'échange de bons procédés entre nos législateurs. Les protectionnistes ayant voté en faveur de la construction de lignes de chemins de fer ou d'autres largesses du gouvernement, dont avaient profité certains libres-échangistes, ceux-ci avaient contracté une dette qu'ils devaient payer.

La classe gouvernementale s'énerve dans cette hypocrisie, dans ces mensonges de chaque jour, dans ces continuelles intrigues parlementaires. Elle n'entend que l'écho de ses propres idées, ne voit rien au-delà, et se figure que le monde parlementaire est la nation. Eloignant ses meilleurs hommes du pouvoir, se partageant cyniquement le produit de spoliations sans cesse croissantes, plus elle rend son joug pesant, et moins elle devient capable de le défendre.

Quand, au milieu de l'indifférence et de l'abstention du plus grand nombre des électeurs, elle a réussi à faire élire par ses paysans, quelque député assez nul et assez ignorant pour pouvoir espérer de s'en faire un instrument aveugle et docile, quand, profitant de l'ignorance des uns, de l'ambition et des convoitises des autres, elle a obtenu la majorité dans la Chambre, elle croit que tout est dit, que son pouvoir est définitivement bien assis, que l'heure des revendications populaires ne sonnera jamais. Elle étend et perfectionne chaque jour l'appareil gouvernemental, c'est elle qui crée cette machine immense et compliquée pour changer la distribution naturelle des richesses, pour faire jouir les uns du produit du travail des autres, pour substituer partout à la libre concurrence la réglementation par l'État, et elle se berce de l'espoir qu'elle pourra toujours employer à son profit cette machine, que l'exemple qu'elle donne ne portera pas ses fruits, que ses fétiches politiques la sauveront, et que, pratiquant chaque jour pour son propre compte le socialisme, elle pourra empêcher les autres de s'en servir aussi.

La Cour de cassation de Turin juge que les associations de socialistes sont des associations de malfaiteurs, parce qu'elles ont pour but de prendre aux uns pour donner aux autres; comme si tel exactement n'était pas le but que se proposent les associations, jugées parfaitement licites, qui se constituent en vue d'obtenir des droits protecteurs ou d'autres faveurs de l'État.

Ne voulant pas se donner la peine d'étudier l'économie politique, craignant d'y trouver la condamnation des ses agissements, la classe gouvernementale nie qu'il existe des lois naturelles de la production et de la distribution des richesses; elle tâche de persuader au peuple que l'état peut tout, et après, quand les malheureux en concluent que ce même État peut améliorer leur sort, assurer des salaires élevés aux ouvriers, détruire les funestes effets du vice et de l'ignorance, et faire régner partout le bonheur, elle s'en étonne et s'en indigne comme d'une hérésie.

Ce naif égoïsme, cet aveuglement inconcevable de la classe moyenne en Europe ne permet de voir l'avenir que sous de sombres couleurs; peut-être, bien que maintenant cela semble peu probable, les peuples ouvriront-ils à temps les yeux sur leurs véritables intérèts, peut-être la réaction naîtra-t-elle de l'excès même du mal, mais pour le moment on ne saurait encore apercevoir d'où et comment viendra le salut.

(1891)

L'ÉTATISME EN ITALIE

I.

Un proverbe allemand dit que les arbres empêchent de voir la forêt. C'est ce qui arrive dans
les sciences sociales. Absorbés par la vue des
détails du phénomène, nous négligeons souvent de
nous rendre compte de son ensemble.

Si, réagissant contre cette tendance, et oubliant
pour un moment les questions du jour, questions
qui nous passionnent et qui, pratiquement, sont
en effet souvent des plus importantes, nous portons
notre attention sur l'évolution des sociétés du
continent européen, depuis 1870, pour ne pas re-
monter plus haut, les progrès de l'étatisme et du
socialisme sont manifestes et deviennent réellement
frappants. La marée socialiste monte chaquer jour,
et ce sont les conservateurs eux-mêmes qui s'em-
pressent à l'envi de miner et de détruire les digues
qui la pourraient encore retenir. La centralisation
prépare le socialisme d'état, et celui-ci ouvre la
voie au socialisme populaire.

Relisez de Tocqueville et vous serez frappé de
l'analogie entre la situation de la société à la fin
du dix-huitième siècle et à l'heure présente. Le

même aveuglement des classes dirigeantes qui prépara, alors, la domination des jacobins, prépare maintenant le succès plus ou moins prochain des socialistes. Est-ce un bien, est-ce un mal? Nous n'entendons pas traiter ici cette question; nous voulons seulement étudier certains phénomènes et faire voir les rapports nécessaires qu'ils ont les uns avec les autres.

Ce sont généralement les conservateurs qui accomplissent l'oeuvre de centralisation, sans laquelle le socialisme d'état ne saurait se développer. Un seul pays, l'Angleterre, échappera très probablement à la conquête socialiste, et cela precisément parce que ses classes dirigeantes se sont bien gardées de se laisser entraîner par les dangereuses utopies théoriques qui, unifiant le droit et l'administration, aboutissent à mettre toute la vie sociale sous la dépendance despotique d'un pouvoir central. Le parti conservateur anglais, voulant s'opposer au parti libéral, qui demandait l'autonomie de l'Irlande, n'a rien su trouver de mieux que de réclamer la plus large décentralisation pour toutes les parties du Royaume-Uni. Tiendra-t-il ses promesses? C'est une autre question; mais le seul fait qu'il s'en est servi comme arme de guerre fait voir combien est vivace en Angleterre le sentiment de la liberté et de l'autonomie locale.

Ce sentiment existe encore en Suisse, bien qu'il

soit moins intense qu'autrefois. C'est à lui que le pays doit de jouir d'une prospérité dont on chercherait en vain d'autres exemples sur le continent européen. M. Léon Donnat, dans son livre *La politique expérimentale*, a fort bien expliqué les avantages de "la législation séparée" pour l'Angleterre et la Suisse. Il écrivait en 1885. Depuis lors, l'Angleterre a persévéré dans la voie libérale, et le mouvement de décentralisation s'y est même accentué. En Suisse, au contraire, on observe un mouvement très puissant qui pousse à la centralisation, et le jour n'est peut-être pas loin où l'on pourra craindre que les cantons, dépouillés peu à peu, en faveur du pouvoir central, de toutes leurs attributions, ne perdent jusqu'à l'ombre de la souveraineté et ne deviennent semblables à des préfectures de la république française. Ainsi tomberaient les digues qui, aujourd'hui encore, empêchent que le socialisme ne prospère en Suisse autant qu'il le fait en France. Si le pouvoir central obtient les monopoles des chemins de fer, de la banque, des assurances, sans compter le monopole de l'alcool et bien d'autres encore; si, étant seul riche, il voit toutes les mains se tendre vers lui; s'il édicte seul des lois sur les matières commerciales, civiles et pénales, et seul les fait appliquer par son tribunal suprême; si les moindres objets administratifs, tels que la police des substances alimentaires, sont soustraits à l'action de l'autorité locale, il est clair que celle-ci finira par n'avoir guère plus d'importance qu'elle n'en a dans tout autre état des plus centralisés. Il se peut que les décisions du referendum populaire et la sagesse des hommes d'état viennent enrayer le mouvement. D'autres personnes, plus compétentes que nous, diront si cela est probable ou non. Notre but, ici, est seulement de noter une tendance qui saute aux yeux de l'observateur le plus superficiel, et forme un cas particulier, intéressant, d'un phénomène plus général, qui s'observe dans les états du continent européen.

Le mouvement qui entraîne ces états, et spécialement l'Allemagne et la France, vers le socialisme, est vraiment des plus remarquables. C'est d'abord la protection douanière qui, depuis 1870, s'étend et augmente chaque jour d'intensité. C'est la spoliation organisée en faveur d'une partie de la classe riche. La leçon donnée ainsi au peuple ne sera pas perdue, et un jour viendra où les spoliateurs d'aujourd'hui seront spoliés à leur tour.

A l'ombre de la protection se développent et prospèrent les monopoles privés: les *trusts* et les *pools* aux Etats-Unis, les *Kartelle* en Allemagne, les syndicats, en France. Seule l'Angleterre y échappe, grâce au libre échange.

Ces monopoles privés sont encore plus malfaisants que les monopoles de l'état. M. Jaurès a parfaitement raison de dire qu'en France ce serait un bienfait pour le pays si l'industrie du sucre qui, en fait, est devenue un monopole privé, était exercée exclusivement par l'état. Certaines lois que l'on veut édicter en plusieurs pays sur les assurances auront pour effet de pousser à la constitution de syndicats et de créer des monopoles privés qui prépareront le monopole de l'état.

Les sociétés de secours mutuels fleurissent en Angleterre, et la législation se garde bien de leur mettre des entraves. En Suisse, elles sont gravement menacées par le projet de loi sur l'assurance obligatoire et, encore plus, par un autre projet de loi sur le contrat d'assurance. Quand on aura ainsi réussi à faire disparaitre toutes les sociétés que l'initiative privée a créées et crée chaque jour pour venir en aide aux travailleurs, il sera aisé de proclamer que ceux-ci ne doivent plus avoir d'espoir qu'en l'intervention de l'état.

Mais c'est surtout la famille qui est en butte aux plus vives attaques, non seulement de la part des socialistes, mais encore d'un grand nombre de personnes composant les classes que l'on nomme dirigeantes, bien que, souvent, en réalité, elles ne dirigent rien du tout et se laissent entraîner par un mouvement dont elles semblent n'avoir même pas conscience.

Législation, philanthropie, art, littérature, tout se réunit pour miner la constitution de la famille.

Il ne suffit pas des atteintes qu'on lui porte sous le couvert du "féminisme," il faut encore que, sous les prétextes les plus variés, on enlève l'enfant à l'influence de la mère et du père. L'idéal qu'on s'efforce d'atteindre peu à peu paraît être celui de la *République* de Platon: des enfants qui ne connaîtront ni leur père ni leur mère, et qui seront nourris et élevés par l'état.

Il se peut que, sous cette nouvelle constitution, la société soit heureuse et prospère, mais l'on voudra bien reconnaître que, la famille ayant été jusqu'à présent la base de notre organisation sociale, celle-ci sera entièrement changée le jour où disparaîtra la constitution que la famille a eue jusqu'à présent. Les personnes qui, s'étant bien rendu compte du nouvel état de choses que l'on prépare ainsi, et l'ayant étudié avec soin, le jugent bon et utile, ont parfaitement raison de suivre la voie qui y conduit. Mais que dire des personnes qui, d'un coeur léger, s'engagent dans cette voie, sans se soucier de savoir où elle aboutit, et qui, répudiant énergiquement la fin, acceptent néanmoins, avec enthousiasme, les moyens?

Les sentiments de dignité et de responsabilité que la sélection a développés dans nos races sont honnis par les admirateurs de l'état *éthique.* Ces braves gens ont en commun avec les socialistes l'aversion pour le petit propriétaire, qui cultive son champ sans rien demander à personne. Ecrasé

d'impôts pour subvenir aux dépenses rendues nécessaires par les folies militaires des classes dirigeantes; nourrissant de son travail des fonctionnaires toujours plus nombreux et plus envahis-
sants; faisant les frais de la protection industrielle
et ne tirant que des bénéfices insignifiants ou
nuls de la protection agricole, qui ne profite
qu'aux grands propriétaires; payant de ses deniers le luxe qu'il plaît aux gouvernements de
déployer dans les villes, les petits propriétaires
deviennent de plus en plus les parias de nos
sociétés. On discute, il est vrai, pour savoir si
leur nombre a réellement diminué en France;
mais, en Italie, c'est par milliers qu'ils disparais-
sent.

Ce n'est pas le petit agriculteur qui connaîtra
jamais la journée de huit heures, ce n'est pas sur
lui que l'assurance obligatoire répandra ses bienfaits, ce n'est pas pour alléger son labeur que
l'état interviendra, comme il intervient en faveur
des ouvriers de certaines industries. Que ce petit
propriétaire vende sa terre, qu'il aille dans les
villes augmenter le nombre des prolétaires, et
qu'au lieu de s'acharner à tourner et retourner la
terre, il passe son temps dans les réunions publiques à applaudir les politiciens, et, du même
coup, il deviendra digne de la sollicitude de l'état
éthique et des sympathies des philanthropes.

Mais il ne veut pas. Il s'obstine à ne pas tendre

la main, et à compter sur ses bras plutôt que sur les aumônes de l'état. Cette terre qu'il a reçue de son père, ce champ qu'il a épierré, ces arbres qu'il a plantés, il a la prétention absurde de les laisser à son fils; il aime sa terre et s'y attache comme l'huître à son rocher. Aussi bien voit-on clairement qu'il faudra employer la force pour l'en détacher. C'est a quoi songent un grand nombre de savants. Les uns ont imaginé une théorie qui rend l'état "co-propriétaire" des terres. C'est une fort belle théorie... pour ceux qui la peuvent comprendre; et qui ferait certainement régner l'abondance... si on pouvait labourer la terre avec des abstractions. D'autres veulent confisquer simplement les terres; d'autres encore, plus modérés, se contenteraient de les racheter. Cela peut être juste et *éthique*, mais il est certain que, quand ce sera fait, une grande partie de la population devra émigrer ou mourir de faim.

Bien des gens trouveront que nous exagérons en voyant dans l'étatisme un acheminement au social-isme. Les socialistes, eux, ne s'y trompent pas, et il faut reconnaître que, surtout en ces derniers temps, ils ont su faire preuve d'une sagacité des plus remarquables et d'un flair politique qui dépasse de beaucoup celui de leurs adversaires. Ils acceptent toutes les concessions, sans en mépriser aucune, grande ou petite, mais aussi sans rien rabattre de leurs principes, sans perdre un moment de vue le but auquel ils veulent arriver. Ils sont bien aises de voir que le gros de leur ouvrage est fait par leurs propres adversaires, et ils les encouragent d'un sourire quand ils les voient s'engager dans les sentiers fleuris du socialisme d'état. Ils ne détestent pas trop non plus le "socialisme chrétien," car ils savent bien que, quand le grain sera levé, c'est eux qui le moissonneront.

En attendant que l'étatisme produise son effet principal, on peut observer des effets secondaires, qui paraissent ne jamais manquer. Nous nous proposons ici de les étudier en Italie. C'était, disait-on, pour faire le bonheur du peuple qu'on voulait donner à l'état les chemins de fer et les banques, et le charger de régler la production au moyen de la protection douanière. Eh bien, interrogeons les faits, voyons ce qui est résulté de tout cela, et si le bien-être du peuple s'en est accru ou a diminué.

II.

Le parti qu'on appelait "modéré" en Italie était libéral. Il subissait l'ascendant de son chef, le comte de Cavour, qui était imbu des idées du libéralisme anglais. D'ailleurs, les traditions de la liberté commerciale étaient anciennes en Toscane; ce petit pays avait servi de modèle même à l'Angleterre, et est souvent cité dans les discours des orateurs de la ligue de Cobden.

Le parti modéré eut seulement le tort de trop vouloir centraliser. M. Minghetti, qui en était pourtant un des chefs, avait proposé un système dit des régions, qui aurait fait une large part à l'autonomie locale. Ce système fut repoussé, et il est curieux d'observer qu'on lui opposa des raisons fort semblables à celles qu'on invoque, de nos jours, en Suisse, pour amoindrir l'autorité des cantons. Le parti modéré est maintenant revenu de son erreur, les maux de la centralisation à outrance l'ont assagi, et M. di Rudinì fait de timides tentatives de décentralisation.

Le parti modéré ne succomba pas aux attaques de ses adversaires; il se détruisit lui-même, en se divisant en deux tronçons dont l'un demeurait fidèle aux doctrines libérales, tandis que l'autre versait de plus en plus dans les théories du socialisme d'état. Les événements de 1870 précipitèrent le mouvement. Beaucoup de jeunes gens allèrent étudier dans les universités allemandes; ils en revinrent imbus des principes de l'économie politique historique ou du socialisme de la chaire, et rêvant de les appliquer en Italie. Naples avait une école de philosophie hégélienne qui, indépendamment, arrivait au même résultat. Silvio Spaventa fut des représentants les plus distingués des tendances économiques de cette école. C'était un parfait honnête homme, suivant les principes d'une morale austère; et pourtant, sans le vouloir, il fut un des facteurs de l'immoralité qui, grâce au socialisme d'état, a envahi peu à peu toute l'administration en Italie. En Piémont, Quintino Sella, homme essentiellement pratique, représentait les anciennes tendances autoritaires, qui, un moment écartées par le comte de Cavour, reparurent après la mort de cet homme d'état. Le Piémont avait une bureaucratie en bien des points semblable a la bureaucratie prussienne. Le grand tort de Quintino Sella fut de ne pas comprendre qu'un mécanisme adapté à un état despotique ne pouvait guère bien fonctionner sous un régime au moins en partie démocratique. Enfin Marco Minghetti, homme d'un grand talent, mais versatile à l'excès, honnête au fond, mais éprouvant le besoin de ne jamais rester avec la minorité, donna son appui aux nouvelles doctrines simplement parce qu'il les crut destinées à triompher. Comme le Jupiter de l'*Iliade*, il pesa les sorts de la liberté et de l'étatisme, et, ce dernier lui ayant paru l'emporter, il se tourna contre les libéraux.

Quelques hommes du parit modéré demeurèrent pourtant fidèles aux doctrines libérales. Un des principaux fut Ubaldino Peruzzi, qui avait fait partie du ministère du comte de Cavour, et qui, jusqu'à sa mort, défendit avec talent et courage la cause de la liberté. Parmi les vivants, on peut citer le marquis Alfieri, qui n'a jamais manqué de combattre pour la liberté économique, et qui, à peu

près seul de son parti, a eu le courage de stigma-
tiser publiquement les méfaits du gouvernement
de M. Crispi.

La bataille décisive pour la cause libérale se
donna au sujet des chemins de fer. Quintino Sella
était favorable à l'exploitation de l'état. Marco
Minghetti ne voulut pas se laisser devancer et,
étant ministre, il proposa, en 1876, le rachat par
l'état des lignes existantes. Les libéraux, Ubaldino
Peruzzi à leur tête, fondèrent alors a Florence la
société *Adam Smith* pour combattre l'étatisme.
Ayant fait partie nous-même de cette société, nous
pouvons en parler en connaissance de cause. On
s'y faisait l'illusion de pouvoir renouveler en
Italie l'oeuvre de la ligue de Cobden en Angleterre. Helas! il était trop tard. L'unification du
droit et de l'administration, que les libéraux
avaient eu le tort énorme d'accomplir, avait déjà
donné un tel pouvoir au gouvernement central,
qu'il était devenu impossible de lui résister. Il
n'est pas facile de trouver des gens disposés à
sacrifier leur avenir et celui de leur famille pour
le triomphe d'un principe. Là où le gouvernement
central est tout-puissant, il n'y a plus que deux
partis, et ils sont divisés non par des idees, mais
par des intérêts matériels. Un des partis jouit de
tous les avantages du pouvoir, l'autre l'en veut
déposséder pour jouir à son tour. Les contribuables paient les frais de la guerre. Nous avons vu

bien des gens qui se prétendaient libéraux, et qui avaient fait partie de la société *Adam Smith*, déserter la cause de la liberté pour obtenir les faveurs du gouvernement. La démocratie libérale et la centralisation sont deux choses incompatibles.

Les raisons que l'on donnait alors en faveur de l'exploitation des chemins de fer par l'état étaient les mêmes que celles qu'on invoque toujours en cette occurrence. D'abord; "Les chemins de fer italiens aux Italiens!" ce sont de belles paroles, mais les gains malhonnêtes qu'elles servirent à recouvrir, et qui furent payés par les contribuables, sont moins dignes de louanges. Dès l'année 1873, une commission parlementaire faisait observer que le rachat des chemins de fer de la Haute-Italie était un acheminement "au rachat des grands travaux publics, dont il est désirable que l'exploitation soit confiée à des intérêts nationaux."[1]

Maintenant, si l'on veut savoir de quels intérêts il s'agissait en réalité, il suffit de prendre connaissance du rapport de la commission d'enquête sur les constructions de chemins de fer qu'a fait exécuter l'état depuis 1879. Ce rapport, qui vient d'être publié, fait voir clairement que le trésor

---

1 "Parve alla giunta che sia questo il primo passo in una buona via, la quale, coll'aiuto del tempo e delle circostanze, dovrà condurre il governo italiano al riscatto di quelle grandi opere pubbliche il cui esercizio è desiderabile rimanga affidato ad interessi nazionali."

public a été soumis à un pillage en régle. C'est ainsi que 514 kilomètres de chemins de fer, que différents entrepreneurs s'étaient engagés à construire pour 202,895,029 francs, finirent par coûter 352,912,750 francs, grâce aux transactions que l'état dut faire plus ou moins volontairement avec ces messieurs. Un tunnel que des entrepreneurs s'étaient engagés à percer pour le prix de 14,178,750 *lires* coûta à l'état près de 43 millions. Les entrepreneurs reçurent 23 millions pour 5,800 mètres de tunnel qu'il avaient effectivement percés; ils surent se faire adjuger dix millions d'indemnité pour les 2500 mètres qu'ils n'avaient pas percés; et enfin, de guerre lasse, l'état dut charger la Compagnie des chemins de fer de la Méditerranée de faire l'ouvrage et lui payer dix millions de ce chef. L'histoire de la construction du chemin de fer de Florence à Vaglia est des plus instructives et riche en incidents piquants. C'est ainsi que, le gouvernement ayant chargé une commission d'examiner sur les lieux certains travaux, le conseil supérieur des travaux publics est trompé (la commission d'enquête ne dit pas par qui), et on lui fait accroire que la nécessité de reconstruire 430 mètres d'un tunnel avait été reconnue par la commission "et surtout par celui des membres de cette commission qui était spécialement compétent pour juger de la nature du sol." Or ce membre affirme, de la manière la plus catégorique, qu'il n'y a pas un mot de vrai en cela.[1]

La commission d'enquête fait observer qu'en général les projets étaient mal étudiés. Ils donnaient ainsi lieu à d'innombrables contestations, qui servaient de prétexte aux entrepreneurs pour rançonner l'état. Celui-ci, d'ailleurs, y mettait de la bonne volonté, et la commission d'enquête note la facilité excessive avec laquelle le gouvernement accueillait les demandes qui lui étaient faites. Cédant à des influences politiques et électorales, bien des ministres des travaux publics, en Italie, paraissent ne s'être souciés que d'accroître les gains des entrepreneurs, qui savaient acheter à beaux deniers comptants les faveurs des politiciens. Heureusement, un homme honnête et énergique, M. Prinetti, est maintenant ministre, et il a entrepris de nettoyer les étables d'Augias, mais il n'est pas sûr que de puissantes influences ne parviennent à le briser avant que son oeuvre soit achevée. Le 11 décembre 1896 il disait à la chambre qu'une longue et patiente étude des faits l'avait conduit à reconnaître que "l'habilité avec laquelle les entrepreneurs marchaient à la con-

---

1 *Relazione della commissione d'inchiesta*, p. 114: "Ora l'ing. Mazzuoli afferma nel modo più risoluto che le cose suesposte non sono conformi al vero, ed avvalora queste sue affermazioni comunicando alla Commissione quello fra i libretti dei suoi appunti che comprende la detta visita."

quête des deniers publics n'avait d'égale que l'insuffisance de la défense." Il ajoutait que bien souvent en Italie l'administration avait été mise au service de la politique, ce qu'il n'entendait plus permettre, au moins dans son ministère. Cette attitude énergique a suffi pour faire réduire spontanément à plusieurs entrepreneurs leurs prétentions à des indemnités absolument fantastiques, que d'autres ministres auraient certainement admises. Les entrepreneurs font actuellement des procès à l'état en demandant des indemnités dont le total est de près de 170 millions. M. Prinetti estime que l'état ne doit que 30 millions; et il est fort probable qu'en définitive la somme à payer ne sera guère plus considérable, si M. Prinetti continue à défendre avec énergie les droits de l'état. C'est ainsi qu'un entrepreneur qui, défendu par un célèbre politicien, demandait 3 millions, a été réduit par M. Prinetti à se contenter de 400,000 francs. Un autre, au lieu de onze millions auxquels il prétendait, fut tout heureux d'en recevoir trois. Un individu, aimé des dieux de l'Olympe, réclamait cinq millions pour son palais exproprié à Naples; M. Prinetti découvrit que, suivant la loi de 1890, la somme due ne dépassait pas deux millions. Cette danse des millions, les libéraux l'avaient prévue dès 1876. Ils faisaient tort, disait-on alors, à l'état *éthique*. Il est facile de voir maintenant à qui les faits ont donné raison.

On nous parlait, ensuite, des bienfaits que l'exploitation des chemins de fer par l'état devait procurer à la production nationale. Les actionnaires des chemins de fer n'avaient pour but que de grossir leurs dividendes; l'état songerait avant tout à l'avenir économique du pays. On promettait même, dans un avenir plus ou moins éloigné, de réduire les tarifs des chemins de fer au simple prix coûtant du transport.[1]

Les beaux discours! Autant en a emporté le vent. Quand le gouvernement eut racheté les chemins de fer, il se garda bien de réduire les tarifs, ou ne fit que des réductions insignifiantes. Maintenant que les chemins de fer sont exploités par des sociétés fermières, l'état, de crainte de voir diminuer la participation qu'il a dans le produit brut, s'oppose à maintes réductions de tarifs proposées par les sociétés. C'est lui qui doit fournir les wagons aux sociétés fermières; aussi font-ils sou-

---

1 M. Boselli, qui était venu défendre l'oeuvre du gouvernement devant la société *Adam Smith*, disait: "Intanto vi è un limite minimo nelle tariffe al quale una società non è obbligata di scendere, ed a cui deve invece discendere il governo.... In questi trasporti nulla guadagna l'esercizio ferroviario, ma guadagna il paese. Quanto al limite massimo delle tariffe, fino al giorno in cui possano queste corrispondere alla semplice spesa del trasporto, è cosa da discutersi in relazione alle condizioni finanziarie del paese."

vent défaut. Depuis plusieurs années, les wagons manquent pour les arrivages dans le port de Gênes, et ce n'est que maintenant que, la situation étant devenue absolument intolérable, l'état a consenti à en acheter de nouveaux. Les admirateurs de l'état éthique seraient bien embarrassés de citer des faits semblables en Angleterre, où le commerce et l'industrie sont sous "la tyrannie" de l'exploitation privée des chemins de fer. Les agriculteurs devaient surtout être favorisés par l'exploitation de l'état. Il est entendu que tout politicien soucieux de ses intérêts doit parler beaucoup des "souffrances de l'agriculture" et promettre d'y porter remède. Nous ignorons si les cultivateurs italiens ont jamais vraiment cru a ces belles promesses; mais, en tout cas, ils attendent encore sous l'orme qu'elles se réalisent, et, pour tout soulagement, ils n'ont eu que de nouveaux impôts à payer.

Après le rachat des chemins de fer de la Haute-Italie et des chemins de fer romains, on eut une période d'exploitation directe par l'état. Ce fut un beau gâchis. Les places dans l'administration des chemins de fer se donnaient sur les recommandations des députés; tout ami des politiciens voyageait gratis; les trains directs devaient s'arrêter à des gares insignifiantes pour flatter l'amour-propre des électeurs de quelque député influent, et l'on achetait les locomotives, les wagons, les rails et le charbon en suivant des principes qui étaient loin d'être ceux de la plus stricte économie. Pour mettre fin à ce désordre, l'exploitation des chemins de fer fut donnée à des compagnies fermières. Nous ignorons si le remède n'a pas été pire que le mal. Bien des abus ont continué, par le fait que l'état est le propriétaire des lignes, et qu'il a la haute main sur toute l'administration des chemins de fer.

Les spéculateurs privés, que les admirateurs de l'état éthique voulaient mettre à la raison, ont commencé par gagner au rachat; ils ont ensuite fait des gains fort considérables lorsque furent approuvées les conventions qui livraient les chemins de fer aux compagnies fermières. Un agiotage effréné, auquel ne manquèrent pas de prendre part les bons législateurs, et peut-être même quelque ministre, envahit tout le pays et créa des fortunes scandaleuses. On n'aurait pas vu de tels faits se produire si l'on avait suivi les conseils des libéraux, qui voulaient laisser les chemins de fer à l'industrie privée. En réalité, ce sont les socialistes d'état qui, voulant combattre les spéculateurs, les ont favorisés, et qui, voulant réprimer l'agiotage, l'ont encouragé.

III.

Si les effets directs des conventions des chemins de fer ne furent guère favorables au pays, les effets indirects furent encore plus nuisibles. L'heureuse issue d'une compagnie où l'intrigue et la corruption parlementaire avaient eu une part prépondérante fut d'un très mauvais exemple. Plusieurs personnes s'étaient enrichies par ce moyen; beaucoup d'autres les voulurent imiter. On ne rêva plus qu'entreprises subventionnées par l'état, que gains faciles obtenus par le pillage des deniers publics; les capitaux délaissèrent les entreprises saines et honnêtes pour se porter vers celles qui, patronnées par des intrigants politiques, promettaient des gains aussi prompts que considérables. Dès lors, tout ministère désireux de se maintenir au pouvoir dut s'ingénier pour trouver de nouvelles spéculations à jeter en pâture à la tourbe famélique des politiciens et de leurs protégés.

On leur servit d'abord une augmentation des droits protecteurs. Ah! ce fut alors le bon temps pour plus d'un député et plus d'un journaliste! Ces droits, comme on peut bien penser, ne s'obtenaient pas gratis, et seules les personnes qui surent se montrer généreuses méritèrent d'être protégées. Certes, il y eut en outre beaucoup de protectionnistes honnêtes et de fort bonne foi.

Tels furent plusieurs savants, entraînés par les doctrines du socialisme de la chaire et de l'étatisme. Ils nous accusaient, nous, économistes libéraux, d'être les adeptes d'une science impitoyable, qui comptait pour rien les souffrances du peuple, et ils nous dépeignaient comme des doctrinaires toujours prêt à sacrifier à des principes abstraits le bonheur et la prospérité du pays.

Eh bien, ils ont pu appliquer leurs théories, il leur a été loisible de faire ce bonheur, de réaliser cette prospérité. A quoi ont-ils abouti? A la ruine du pays et à la misère du peuple.

Quelques chiffres donnent éloquemment la synthèse de ces faits. Le savant directeur de la statistique italienne, M. Bodio, a calculé la moyenne des salaires d'un grand nombre d'ouvriers et en a déduit le nombre d'heures de travail qui leur était nécessaire pour se procurer 100 kilogrammes de froment. En 1881, ce nombre d'heures était de 122; sous l'empire de la demi-liberté économique dont jouissait l'Italie, ce nombre va en diminuant graduellement, et n'est plus que de 93 heures en 1886. Mais, en 1887, la scène change; l'état *éthique* veut, au moyen de la protection, faire fleurir l'agriculture et l'industrie, il pousse à une augmentation insensée de constructions, de nouveaux édifices, et étend sa sollicitude paternelle jusqu'aux banques, qu'il dépouille. Le nombre d'heures de travail nécessaires pour acheter 100 kilos de froment remonte alors graduellement et atteint, en 1891, le chiffre de 101. Si c'est là faire le bonheur des travailleurs, il faut avouer que, pour rendre ce bonheur parfait, on n'aurait qu'à les faire tous mourir d'inanition.

Qu'il nous soit permis de citer ici quelques passages d'un article que nous écrivions, en 1887, dans le *Journal des Economistes* sur le nouveau tarif douanier italien. Bien des faits se sont passés depuis cette époque; ils ont confirmé entièrement nos déductions, et nous n'avons pas un seul mot á changer à se que nous nous disions alors:

"Il y avait autrefois en Italie un impôt sur la mouture des céréales, établi en 1868 par un ministère de droite. C'était le temps où il y avait encore une droite et une gauche dans notre parlement, et celle-ci tonnait fort contre cet impôt antidémocratique, qui faisait renchérir le pain du *pauvre peuple;* car il paraît qu'alors la théorie et la pratique allaient d'accord pour reconnaître qu'une taxe sur la farine augmente le prix du pain; maintenant, nous avons changé tout cela. La gauche donc réclamait à cor et à cri le dégrèvement de la mouture; c'était son *delenda Carthago,* l'arme avec laquelle elle sapait le pouvoir des ministères de droite. Enfin, en 1876, la gauche vint au pouvoir; et, comme on avait encore alors le préjugé que les hommes doivent mettre une certaine suite entre leurs discours et leurs actes, on abolit effectivement l'impôt sur la mouture, en 1880.

"Depuis, les hommes de la gauche se faisaient gloire d'avoir dégrevé le pain du pauvre, et cela continua jusqu'à tout récemment; il y eut même des retardataires, parmi lesquels des ministres, qui déclaraient que 'jamais' ils n'auraient consenti à l'augmentation des droits sur le blé; malheureusement, ce jamais ne dura que fort peu de jours, et, le 18 avril 1881, ces mêmes ministres présentaient à la chambre le projet de loi qui augmentait le droit d'entrée sur les céréales. Il est vrai qu'au cours de la discussion, le ministre du commerce déclarait que le droit de 3 francs les 100 kilos n'était que fiscal, se séparant en cela de son collègue le ministre des finances et du rapporteur de la commission parlementaire, qui admettaient bel et bien la protection.[1]

"Aux droits protecteurs viennent s'ajouter les droits d'octroi que les communes ont mis sur la

---

1 Le 10 février 1888, ce droit fut porté à 5 francs; le 21 janvier 1894, à 7 francs; le 10 décembre 1894, à 7 fr. 50; et M. Sonnino, déposant le masque philantropique dont il aimait autrefois à recouvrir ses amours avec le socialisme de la chaire, déclarait brutalement que l'établissement de ce droit ne soulevait qu'une question d'intérêt entre différentes classes sociales. En fait de protection, il n'y a que le premier pas qui coûte, comme le dit fort bien M. Numa Droz: "Le protectionnisme, comme tout principe faux, n'a pas en lui-même de pondération. Lorsqu'on a augmenté les droits, il faut les augmenter encore, et cela indéfiniment."

farine. Ces droits, qui en plusieurs localités sont très considérables, n'ont pas été une des moindres causes des mouvements insurrectionnels en Sicile.

"Une terrible maladie, la *pellagre*, est la conséquence de l'alimentation exclusive avec le maïs; elle a diminué quand le prix du froment baissait, elle augmentera s'il renchérit, et, si même elle restait stationnaire, ce n'est vraiment pas là un état de choses qui mérite qu'on tâche de le consolider. Ceux qui réclament l'intervention de l'état en toute chose devraient bien se rappeler que c'est précisément parce qu'il fait augmenter le prix du blé, au profit des propriétaires, que des malheureux sont décimés par la *pellagre*, et bien souvent conduits ainsi à la démence et au suicide."

Le nombre de morts causées par la *pellagre* était de 1698 en 1884; il tombe à 1182 en 1887; mais en 1891, grâce aux progrés de la protection et de l'étatisme, il augmente de nouveau et atteint 1606.

Le jour n'est pas encore venu pour raconter l'histoire de la fondation de certains établissements protégés par le gouvernement; quand cette histoire pourra être connue dans tous ses détails, on verra un curieux contraste entre les gains illicites de la protection et les maux qui en ont été la conséquence.

IV.

La rupture des rapports commerciaux avec la France avait été fort nuisible à l'agriculture italienne, qui trouvait en France un large débouché pour ses produits. Il était donc évident, pour tout observateur impartial, que le pays allait à l'encontre d'une crise économique, et que le moment était venu de se recueiller et d'arrêter la progression toujours croissante des dépenses publiques et des immobilisations de capitaux. Au contraire, on parut n'avoir d'autre souci que de donner un nouvel essor à ces dépenses. Pour y faire face, on eut recours aux banques d'émission. Sous la pression exercée par le gouvernement, celles-ci durent peu à peu immobiliser tous leurs capitaux, pour subventionner les entreprises qui n'avaient à peu près d'autres ressources que celles que leur procurait l'escompte de traites sans cesse renouvelées. On édifiait ainsi des châteaux de cartes que le moindre souffle de vent devait jeter par terre. Ce fut la cause principale de la ruine des banques d'émission. Les vols et les malversations des politiciens n'eurent pour effet que d'accélérer la crise: elles furent la goutte d'eau qui fait déborder le vase.

Les personnes qui veulent faire intervenir l'état dans l'administration des banques d'émission s'imaginent qu'il suffit de régler savamment cette intervention pour obtenir des bons résultats. "Que craignez-vous, disent-elles, pour le portefeuille des banques, si celles-ci ne peuvent escompter que des effets à trois mois, revêtus de trois signatures?" Telles étaient les dispositions de la loi italienne, mais cela n'empêcha nullement les banques de remplir leurs portefeuilles de fort mauvais papier, qu'au moyen d'artifices plus ou moins ingénieux on renouvelait incessamment. On jugeait du degré de confiance que méritaient les signatures, non d'après la solvabilité, mais d'après les recommandations des ministers; ce qui est loin d'être la même chose.

Quant à la surveillance des banques d'emission, elle était on ne peut mieux organisée. Tout y était prévu, au moins sur le papier, et un luxe de précautions des plus minutieuses devait empêcher tout abus.

Les banques d'émission, comme les autres sociétés anonymes, ont leurs censeurs nommés par l'assemblée des actionnaires, et dont le devoir est de surveiller l'administration. En outre, l'article 177 du code de commerce prescrit que, dans les premiers huit jours de chaque mois, les banques doivent déposer au greffe du tribunal de commerce la situation de leur bilan. Cette situation doit être établie sur un modèle fixé par décret royal, et être certifiée conforme à la vérité par un des administrateurs et par un des censeurs.

Enfin, le gouvernement avait soin de publier chaque mois un bulletin contenant ces bilans des banques d'émission. Ces détails sont déjà admirablement réglés; pourtant, la sollicitude du gouvernement ne s'en était pas contentée. Un Argus spécial, sous le nom de commissaire royal, était attaché à chaque banque, avec la mission exclusive d'en surveiller l'administration. Enfin, le gouvernement faisait faire en outre, de temps à autre, des inspections extraordinaires. Cette minutieuse surveillance n'était pas sans coûter cher aux contribuables, mais, au moins, ils étaient bien renseigné. Oui, si la surveillance était effective; mais si elle ne l'était pas? *Sed quis custodiet ipsos custodes?* L'Argus de la fable ne put réussir à bien garder la chasteté d'Io; les Argus du gouvernement n'ont pas mieux gardé l'honnêteté des banques d'émission.

L'Italie avait six banques d'émission; quatre, c'est-à-dire la *Banca Nazionale*, la *Banca Toscana*, la *Banca Toscana di Credito*, la *Banca Romana* sont des sociétés anonymes; deux, c'est-à-dire le *Banco* de Naples et le *Banco* de Sicile, sont de pures banques d'état sans actionnaires. Ces deux dernières banques furent parmi les plus éprouvées; au contraire, la *Banca Toscana di Credito*, pour laquelle, en fait, l'ingérence de l'état se trouvait réduite au minimum, a été le seule bien administrée et qui ait toujours eu une bonne situation financière.

Suivant le rapport de la commission d'enquête présidée par le sénateur Finali, la Banque nationale, avec un capital de 190 millions, en avait immobilisé 142. Le détail de ces immobilisations est instructif:

Immeubles pour bureaux		12 197 106
Autres immeubles		1 279 635
Subvention à la *Banca Tiberina*		45 001 378
" à la société de l'*Esquilino*		5 553 746
" à la *Compagnie Foncière*		18 598 783
" aux compagnies associées à la *Foncière*		8 675 757
" à la Société *de construction de Naples*		15 759 000
" à la *Banque populaire* de Turin (en liquidation)		1 784 312
" à la société du *Crédit méridional*		1 889 000
" à la Banque *agricole de la Basilicata*		7 281 300
" à M. Diana		3 467 833
" à un propriétaire		1 500 000
Crédits hypothécaires		19 643 239
Total		142 641 089

Il résulte de l'enquête que les immobilisations pour la banque *Tiberina*, pour l'*Esquilino*, pour la *Fonciére* et ses associées, pour la *Banque populaire* de Turin, furent imposées par le gouvernement. Les Argus durent naturellement fermer les yeux.

Le procès-verbal du conseil d'administration

du *Banco* de Naples, en date du 31 août 1889, est curieux à consulter. Le directeur du *Banco*, M. le comte Giusso, expose qu'il a dû prendre part à une réunion dans le cabinet du président du conseil des ministres, à laquelle sont intervenus les ministres des finances, le directeur de la Banque nationale et les directeurs de la banque *Tiberina* et de la banque *Sconto e Sete* de Turin. "Le but de cette réunion était de délibérer sur les moyens de venir en aide aux banques turinoises et surtout à la banque *Tiberina*, qui était celle qui intéressait le plus le gouvernement." Le comte Giusso refusa les 25 millions qu'on demandait au *Banco* de Naples pour venir en aide aux entreprises auxquelles "s'intéressait le gouvernement." Ce refus ne demeura pas impuni: le gouvernement ôta à cet honnête homme la direction du *Banco*. Aussi les dilapidations reprirent-elles de plus belle, et les plus récentes occupent maintenant l'attention des tribunaux italiens. Or, il est évident qu'on aurait coupé le mal à sa racine, si l'on avait, une fois pour toutes, soustrait l'administration du *Banco* de Naples aux influences politiques. M. Luzzatti s'est plaint à la chambre de ce qu'il s'était formé dans le pays des association ayant pour but de dépouiller les banques d'émission. Mais comment se fait-il qu'aucune association de ce genre n'ose s'attaquer ni à la Banque d'Angleterre, ni à la Banque de France?

L'histoire de la Banque romaine est tout simplement merveilleuse. Un rapport présenté le 15
mars 1875 à la chambre des députés se plaint
déjà des graves irrégularités de l'administration
de cette banque. Elle avait racheté une partie de
ses actions et, ajoute le rapport, "ce qui est pire,
c'est que son capital n'existe plus qu'en apparence,
car il s'est formé un déficit de beaucoup supérieur. Depuis la fondation de la banque, des effets
étaient tombés en souffrance pour des sommes
considérables, et, au lieu de les passer au compte
des pertes, on les avait portés à l'actif du bilan
pour leur pleine valeur, de sorte que, lorsqu'après
l'année 1870 on voulut changer de système, on
dut réduire la valeur d'un grand nombre de ces
effets du 50 et même du 75 pour cent." Les Argus
sommeillaient, les politiciens besoigneux se faisaient prêter de l'argent par la Banque romaine,
dont, naturellement, la condition continuait à
empirer. Un nouveau rapport, présenté à la chambre le 21 février 1879, fait allusion à cette banque
en disant que "les difficultés dans lesquelles se
débattent quelques-unes des banques de moindre
importance pourraient conduire à des vrais désastres, si l'on n'y portait remède au plus tôt."
Malgré cela, dix ans se passent sans que l'on songe
le moins du monde à ce remède. Enfin, en 1889,
la situation de la Banque romaine est devenue
intolérable; elle peut de moins en moins changer

ses billets. Le gouvernement se décide à agir; il ordonne une enquête extraordinaire. L'enquête faite, les résultats en sont tenus secrets. Quelques politiciens seuls en ont connaissance et ils en profitent, ainsi que l'ont prouvé des documents présentés à la chambre et publiés par M. Cavallotti, pour se faire prêter de l'argent par la Banque romaine.

Ce ne fut qu'en 1893 qu'on connut les résultats de l'enquête dont nous venons de parler: ils sont vraiment fort graves. Il y avait une circulation clandestine de 25 millions de francs. Toute l'administration de la banque était dans le plus grand désordre. Depuis cinq années on n'avait plus vérifié la caisse; et le sénateur Alvisi, rapporteur de la commission d'enquête, concluait en disant: "La comptabilité est mal tenue; la création des billets est anormale; leur circulation excessive et en partie dissimulée; la caisse est mal tenue; les billets en réserve sont mal gardés, ansi que les billets neufs, destinés au change des anciens, et de ceux qui sont prêts pour de nouvelles émissions illégitimes et illégales."

Le dénouement est connu. La Banque romaine dut être liquidée; le directeur, M. Tanlongo, fut emprisonné, mais absous par les jurés. Ceux-ci eurent probablement pitié de ce vieillard dont on voulait faire un bouc émissaire. Il était certainement coupable; mais il le parut moins que les politiciens qui avaient exploité la banque, et qui l'on se gardait bien de poursuivre.

Au moins, en sacrifiant les banques d'émission, a-t-on évité la crise économique? a-t-on sauvé d'autres entreprises? Pas le moins du monde. La crise a été aggravée, toutes les entreprises qu'on voulait sauver tombées. La *Tiberina*, la *Foncière*, l'*Immobiliare*, le *Risanamento*, la *Banque générale*, le *Crédit mobilier*, l'*Esquilino*, la *Cassa sovvenzioni*, et bien d'autres sociétés encore, tout a disparu. On dirait un vaste champ de bataille, où il ne reste plus que des morts et des blessés. M. Luzzatti disait dernièrement à la chambre que ces désastres étaient dus à une sorte de "folie collective des Italiens." C'est se payer de mots que de raisonner ainsi. La seule et vraie cause de ces désastres, c'est l'étatisme, c'est la fraude et la corruption, qui en sont la conséquence; l'agiotage et la spéculation substitués aux honnêtes labeurs de l'agriculture, de l'industrie et du commerce. La folie, si folie il y a, a atteint exclusivement les politiciens, car le peuple n'a rien eu à voir dans tout cela. Il n'a d'ailleurs que trop peu de part au gouvernement pour qu'on puisse même l'accuser de s'être laissé tromper par ces beaux parleurs, qui prétendaient vouloir faire le bonheur du pays au moyen d'un gouvernement paternel, tandis qu'ils ne vivaient en réalité que des gains malhonnêtes de la protection. En tout cas, les économistes libéraux ont echappé entièrement à la pretendue folie collective dont on nous parle maintenant; ils n'ont pas eu de peine à prévoir les effets de l'étatisme en Italie, car ils n'avaient pour cela qu'à se rappeler ceux qu'il avait produits en d'autres contrées. En 1887, lorsque nous publiions l'article que nous avons cité, les protectionnistes répétaient sur tous les tons que le nouveau tarif douanier italien devait faire le prospérité du pays. Nous disions précisément le contraire. On peut voir maintenant à qui les faits ont donné raison.

La crise des banques d'émission en Italie est loin d'être terminée. De temps à autre on tâche d'y porter remède par de nouvelles lois, qui, en pratique, se trouvent être tout aussi inefficaces que les anciennes. Il n'y aurait qu'une manière de mettre un terme à la crise: ce serait de liquider entièrement les opérations irrégulières qui ont été faites jusqu'à ce jour, et de reconstituer les banques d'émission sur le modèle des institutions analogues qui donnent de bons résultats en Angleterre et en France.

V.

On connaît le conte si souvent répété de ce magicien qui, après avoir invoqué le diable, ne savait comment faire pour s'en débarrasser, ayant oublié la formule pour le chasser. Une aventure à peu près semblable est arrivée aux étatistes italiens. Ce sont eux qui ont principalement aidé à la propagation du socialisme, et maintenant ils en sont épouvantés et ne savent plus comment s'y prendre pour l'arrêter.

Une oligarchie militaire, telle que celle qui régit l'Allemagne, peut, à la rigueur, se passer la fantaisie de faire des expériences étatistes; seul l'avenir, pourtant, dira si ce qui est sans danger aujourd'hui le sera toujours; mais, dans une démocratie, l'étatisme aboutit nécessairement à une corruption politique qui infecte tout le pays. C'est une erreur de croire que les qualités morales d'une nation pourront corriger les vices du système. Ainsi, avant 1860, le Piémont était le modèle des états constitutionnels. L'election des députés s'y faisait d'une manière honnête et loyale, et la corruption électorale était nulle ou insignifiante. Une trentaine d'années ont suffi pour changer entièrement cet état de choses. Les élections sont devenues un marché; le candidat paie son élection argent comptant ou par les faveurs du gouvernement. L'ancienne magistrature du Piémont et de la Toscane était digne des plus grands éloges; aujourd'hui, ses successeurs rendent parfois des services au lieu d'arrêts.

Une des conséquences les plus déplorables de ces abus, c'est que le peuple perd chaque jour

davantage le respect dû à l'autorité et aux magistrats, et l'on ne peut qu'être effrayé en songeant
à l'anarchie morale qui envahit ainsi le pays.
Ecoutez un homme du peuple qui a essuyé quelque injustice ; il n'invoque ni son droit ni l'équité,
il ne pense pas plus aux tribunaux que s'ils
n'existaient point ; c'est seulement la protection
de quelque politicien influent qu'il invoque, et,
si celle-ci lui fait défaut, c'est à la violence qu'il
sera tenté de recourir.

La corruption du gouvernement n'est que trop
réelle, mais elle est encore amplifiée par la fantaisie populaire, qui juge que rien ne se donne
et ne s'obtient si ce n'est par la faveur. N'a-t-on
pas vu jusqu'à des élèves des écoles secondaires
demander qu'à l'occasion du mariage du prince
de Naples on les considérât comme ayant réussi
dans les examens où ils avaient échoué ?

En Italie, comme en France, tout le monde
aspire à devenir fonctionnaire du gouvernement.
On a beau créer de nouveaux emplois, le plus souvent inutiles, il n'y en a jamais assez pour contenter tous les candidats. Les ministres se plai-
gnent de ce que le nombre des déclassés va
toujours en augmentant ; mais à qui la faute vraiment, si ce n'est à l'état, qui a voulu absorber
toute la vie économique du pays ? Le mécontente-
ment est général, et le gouvernement est souvent
accusé à tort pour des faits auxquels il n'a pas

la moindre part. Mais cela est naturel; quand on prétend faire le bonheur de tout le monde, quand on veut substituer en tout et pour tout l'action de l'état à l'initiative individuelle, il ne faut pas après s'étonner si chacun rend responsable le gouvernement de ce qui lui arrive de fâcheux dans la vie.

Cet état de choses ne saurait se changer en un jour; ce n'est qu'avec l'aide du temps qu'on peut espérer de le modifier en revenant aux systèmes libéraux que préconisait Cavour, et qu'on a eu grand tort d'abandonner.

Le ministère Rudinì est certainement composé d'honnêtes gens, animés des meilleures intentions, mais jusqu'à présent l'oeuvre de reconstitution morale qu'il a entreprise n'avance guère. Mal soutenu par le roi, qui est intervenu plus d'une fois pour sauver M. Crispi, ne pouvant ainsi arrêter le mal à sa source, il se heurte à des difficultés vraiment inextricables. On a envoyé en Sicile M. Codronchi, avec des pouvoirs étendus, pour mettre un terme aux abus des administrations locales. C'est un homme honnête, actif, énergique, et pourtant son oeuvre jusqu'à présent a été à peu près nulle. Les adversaires du ministère disent que M. Codronchi finira par être simplement le grand électeur du gouvernement en Sicile. Cela pourrait bien être vrai, sans qu'il y eût la faute de personne; tout simplement parce que la ma-

chine du gourvernement fonctionne fort bien lorsqu'il s'agit d'influencer les électeurs, tandis
qu'elle ne fonctionne plus du tout si on veut
l'employer à réprimer et à empêcher les abus et
les malversations.

Le mal ne vient pas directement des hommes
qui sont à la tête du gouvernement, il vient du
système de centralisation et d'intervention de
l'état. C'est ce système qui livre les provinces ita-
liennes à l'exploitation de bandes savamment organisées, de politiciens et d'intrigants. Ce sont
ces bandes qui, à proprement parler, gouvernent
le pays, ce sont elles qui appuient des ministères
tels que celui de M. Crispi, et qui font opposition,
ne fût-ce que par une résistance passive, aux
honnêtes gens, tels que M. di Rudinì. Seule la
liberté économique peut saper les fondements de
leur puissance, la détruire et en délivrer le pays.

(1897)